BlackBerry® Storm™
FOR
DUMMIES®

C.
or
w
w

BlackBerry® Storm™ FOR DUMMIES®

by Robert Kao and Dante Sarigumba

Wiley Publishing, Inc.

BlackBerry® Storm™ For Dummies®

Published by
Wiley Publishing, Inc.
111 River Street
Hoboken, NJ 07030-5774

www.wiley.com

For general information on our other products and services, please contact our Customer Care Department within the U.S. at 877-762-2974, outside the U.S. at 317-572-3993, or fax 317-572-4002.

For technical support, please visit www.wiley.com/techsupport.

Wiley also publishes its books in a variety of electronic formats. Some content that appears in print may not be available in electronic books.

Library of Congress Control Number: 2008943639

ISBN: 978-0-470-42220-5

Manufactured in the United States of America

10 9 8 7 6 5 4 3 2 1

WILEY

About the Authors

Robert Kao is one well-rounded professional. His ability to translate his technical knowledge and communicate with users of all types led him to co-write *BlackBerry For Dummies* and *BlackBerry Pearl For Dummies*. He started out as a BlackBerry developer for various financial firms in New York City, that truly global city. A graduate of Columbia University, with a Computer Engineering degree, he currently lives in South Brunswick, New Jersey.

Dante Sarigumba is a long-time user of BlackBerry and a gizmo enthusiast. He is a co-host of the Mobile Computing Authority biweekly podcast. He works for a major investment bank in New York as a software developer and lives in South Brunswick, New Jersey, with his wife, Rosemarie, and two sons, Dean and Drew.

Dedications

I would like to thank my father (MHK) and mother (SYT) for everything they've done for me. I wouldn't be here without their kindness and support. I would also like to thank my lovely wife, Marie-Claude, and little Jade for all their support.

— Robert Kao

To Yosma, Dean, and Drew: My greatest treasures. Thank you for your thoughts, understanding, and support.

— Dante Sarigumba

Authors' Acknowledgments

Collectively, we want to give a big thanks to Greg Croy for the opportunities to work with the *For Dummies* brand and congratulate him on his retirement! Enjoy it Greg.

In addition, we'd like to thank the following people:

- Katie Mohr, our new acquisitions editor. We look forward to working with you.
- Carol McClendon, our agent, for presenting our proposal to the right people.
- Rebecca Senninger and Tonya Cupp, our editors, for making us look good.
- Victoria Berry, PR of Research In Motion, for getting us access to proper channels at the right time.
- Richard Evers, of Research In Motion, for a wealth of information and guidance.

In addition, we thank the rest of the Wiley staff. Without you all, this book would not have been possible.

— Rob & Dante

Publisher's Acknowledgments

We're proud of this book; please send us your comments through our online registration form located at http://dummies.custhelp.com. For other comments, please contact our Customer Care Department within the U.S. at 877-762-2974, outside the U.S. at 317-572-3993, or fax 317-572-4002.

Some of the people who helped bring this book to market include the following:

Acquisitions and Editorial

Project Editor: Rebecca Senninger

Executive Editor: Greg Croy

Acquisition Editor: Katie Mohr

Copy Editor: Tonya Cupp

Technical Editor: Richard Evers

Editorial Manager: Leah Cameron

Editorial Assistant: Amanda Foxworth

Sr. Editorial Assistant: Cherie Case

Cartoons: Rich Tennant
(www.the5thwave.com)

Composition Services

Project Coordinator: Katherine Key

Layout and Graphics: Carl Byers, Reuben W. Davis, Christin Swinford, Ronald Terry

Proofreaders: Laura Albert, Lynn Stuart

Indexer: Broccoli Information Management

Special Help: Jennifer Riggs

Publishing and Editorial for Technology Dummies

Richard Swadley, Vice President and Executive Group Publisher

Andy Cummings, Vice President and Publisher

Mary Bednarek, Executive Acquisitions Director

Mary C. Corder, Editorial Director

Publishing for Consumer Dummies

Diane Graves Steele, Vice President and Publisher

Composition Services

Gerry Fahey, Vice President of Production Services

Debbie Stailey, Director of Composition Services

Contents at a Glance

Table of Contents

Introduction

Hi there, and welcome to *BlackBerry Storm For Dummies*. If you already have a BlackBerry Storm, this is a great book to have around when you want to discover new features or need something to slap open and use as a quick reference. If you don't have a Storm yet and have some basic questions (such as "What is a BlackBerry Storm?" or "How can a BlackBerry Storm help me be more productive?"), you can benefit by reading this book cover to cover. No matter what your current BlackBerry user status — BUS, for short — we're here to help you get the most out of your BlackBerry Storm.

Right off the bat, we can tell you that a BlackBerry Storm isn't a fruit you find at the supermarket, nor is it related to nasty weather patterns but rather is an always-connected handheld device that has e-mail capabilities and a built-in Internet browser. With your BlackBerry Storm, you're in the privileged position of always being able to receive e-mail and browse the Web.

On top of that, a BlackBerry Storm has all the features you expect from a personal organizer, including a calendar, to-do lists, and memos. Oh, and did we mention that a BlackBerry Storm also has a built-in mobile phone? Talk about multitasking! Imagine being stuck on a commuter train: With your BlackBerry Storm by your side, you can compose e-mail while conducting a conference call — all from the comfort of your seat.

That's not all. BlackBerry Storm goes a step further to make it more fun for you to own this device. You can snap a picture with its camera, record a funny video, listen to your music collection, and enjoy watching that video on YouTube.

In this book, we show you all the basics and then go the extra mile by highlighting some of the lesser-known (but still handy) features of the BlackBerry Storm. Your Storm can work hard for you when you need it to and can play hard when you want it to. (Need we say that we're ready, willing, and able to show you where to get great games for your BlackBerry Storm?)

About This Book

BlackBerry Storm For Dummies is a comprehensive user guide as well as a quick user reference. This book is designed so that you can read it cover to cover if you want, but you don't need to read one chapter after the other.

Feel free to jump around while you explore the different functionalities of your BlackBerry Storm.

We cover basic and advanced topics, but we stick to those that we consider the most practical and frequently used. If you use or want to use a certain function of your BlackBerry Storm, we likely cover it here.

Who Are You?

In this book, we tried to be considerate of your needs, but because we've never met you, our image of you is as follows. If you find that some of these images are true about you, this might just be the book for you:

- You have a BlackBerry Storm and you want to find out how to get the most from it.

- You don't have a BlackBerry Storm yet, and you're wondering what one could do for you.

- You're looking for a book that doesn't assume that you know all the jargon and tech terms used in the PDA industry. (*PDA* stands for *personal digital assistant,* by the way. Take that, you jargon, you!)

- You want a reference that shows you, step by step, how to do useful and cool things with a BlackBerry Storm without bogging you down with unnecessary background or theory.

- You're tired of hauling your ten-pound laptop with you on trips, and you're wondering how to turn your BlackBerry Storm into a miniature traveling office.

- You no longer want to be tied to your desktop system for the critical activities in your life, such as sending and receiving e-mail, checking your calendar for appointments, and surfing the Web.

- You like to have some fun, play games, and be entertained from a device but don't want to carry an extra game gadget on your bag.

What's in This Book

BlackBerry Storm For Dummies consists of five parts, and each part consists of different chapters related to that part's theme.

Part I: Meeting and Greeting Your BlackBerry Storm

Part I starts with the basics of your Storm. You know: What it is, what you can do with it, and what the parts are. We describe how you navigate using the innovative touch screen that behaves like a button and the difference between the QWERTY and SureType keyboard layout. We also show you how to personalize and express yourself through your BlackBerry Storm. This part wraps up with must-knows about security and where to go for help when you get into trouble with your BlackBerry.

Part II: Getting Organized with Your Storm

Part II deals with the fact that your BlackBerry Storm is also a full-fledged PDA. We show you how to get your Storm to keep your contacts in Contacts as well as how to manage your appointments and meetings in Calendar. We also show you how to take notes and do quick arithmetic calculations on your Storm. As you'll see, most BlackBerry applications interconnect, working hard for you.

Part III: Getting Multimedia and Online with Your Storm

Part III shows you what made BlackBerry what it is today — always-connected e-mail. We also get into the other strengths of the BlackBerry — Web surfing functionality — but it doesn't stop there. We also point out how you can use other forms of messages on the BlackBerry that you might not have known about, such as PIN-to-PIN messages. We also describe the fun features of your BlackBerry, such as using its camera, listening to music, and recording and watching videos. And rest assured that your BlackBerry will be a good companion when you're traveling because we also show you how to use its GPS.

Part IV: Working with Desktop Manager

In Part IV, we detail BlackBerry Desktop Manager and show you some of the hoops you can put it through with your BlackBerry Storm, including making backups and installing BlackBerry applications from your PC to your Storm. You also find out how to port data from your older devices — BlackBerry or not — to your new Storm. And we didn't forget to cover important stuff, such as data syncing your appointments and contacts with desktop applications, such as Outlook.

Part V: The Part of Tens

All *For Dummies* books include The Part of Tens, and this book is no different. In Part V, we show you where to get cool BlackBerry Storm accessories, visit useful mobile Web sites, and (of course) get great applications and games to play on your BlackBerry Storm. In addition, we keep this list up-to-date on our Web site at www.blackberryfordummies.com.

Icons in This Book

 This icon highlights an important point that you don't want to forget because it just might come up again. We'd never be so cruel as to spring a pop quiz on you, but paying attention to these details can definitely help you.

 This book rarely delves into the geeky, technical details, but when it does, this icon warns you. Read on if you want to get under the hood a little, or just skip ahead if you aren't interested in the gory details.

 Here's where you can find not-so-obvious tricks that can make you a Black-Berry Storm power-user in no time. Pay special attention to the paragraphs with this icon to get the most out of your Storm.

 Look out! This icon tells you how to avoid trouble before it starts.

Where to Go from Here

If you want to find out more about the book or have a question or comment for the authors, please visit us at any of the following:

- ✔ www.BlackBerryForDummies.com
- ✔ www.BlackBerryGoodies.com — where we answer your submitted questions

Now you can dive in! Give Chapter 1 a quick look to get an idea of where this book takes you and then feel free to head straight to your chapter of choice.

Part I
Meeting and Greeting Your BlackBerry Storm

The 5th Wave   By Rich Tennant

"This model comes with a particularly useful function – a simulated static button for breaking out of long winded conversations."

In this part . . .

The road to a happy and collaborative relationship with your BlackBerry Storm starts here. Chapter 1 covers all the nuts and bolts: how the Storm works, its look and feel, and connectivity. Chapter 2 describes how you navigate through the virtual keys. Chapter 3 discusses customizing your BlackBerry and also how to take care of your device.

Chapter 1

Your BlackBerry Is NOT an Edible Fruit

*B*ecause you're reading this book, you probably have a BlackBerry Storm (and we're pretty sure that you're not eating it). We're just curious, though — what actually convinced you to buy this particular handheld mobile device? Was it the touch screen? Was it the always-connected e-mail? Or the multimedia player to replace your iPod or iPhone? Or was it the really good sales pitch? We know; the list could go on and on — and we might never hit on the exact reason you got yours. For whatever reason you got your BlackBerry, congratulations; you made an intelligent choice.

The same smarts that made you buy your BlackBerry Storm are clearly at it again. This time, your intelligence led you to pick up this book, perhaps because your intuition told you there's more to your BlackBerry Storm than meets the eye.

Your hunch is right. Your Storm *can* help you do more than you supposed. For example, your BlackBerry is a whiz at making phone calls, but it's also a computer that can check your e-mail and surf the Web. We're talking *World Wide* Web here, so the sky's the limit. Help is always at your fingertips rather than sitting on some desk at home or at the office.

✔ Need to check out the reviews of that restaurant on the corner?

✔ Need to know — right now — what's showing in your local movie theaters, or what's coming in the weather tonight, or what's the best place to shop the sales?

✔ Need to know your current location and get directions to that cozy bed and breakfast, or retrieve news headlines, or check stock quotes?

    ✔ Want to do some online chatting or view some pictures online?

    ✔ Hankering to network with your old classmates?

You can do all these things (and more) by using your BlackBerry Storm.

Storm is also a full-fledged *personal digital assistant (PDA)*. Out of the box, it provides you with the organizational tools you need to set up to-do lists, manage your appointments, take care of your address books, and more.

Being armed with a device that's a phone, an Internet connection, a PDA, a GPS, and full-on media player all built into one makes you a powerful person. With your Storm (along with this resourceful book), you really can increase your productivity and become better organized. Watch out, world! BlackBerry Storm-wielding powerhouse coming through!

If you stick with us, you find out all you need to get the most out of your device or maybe even save a troubled relationship. (Well, the last one is a bit of an exaggeration, but we got your attention, right?)

How It All Works: The Schematic Approach

For those who always ask, "How do they do that?" you don't have to go far; this little section is just for you.

The role of the network service provider

Along with wondering how your BlackBerry Storm actually works, you might also be wondering why you didn't get your Storm from RIM rather than from a network service provider such as Cingular or T-Mobile. Why did you need to go through a middle person? After all, RIM makes BlackBerry Storm.

That's an excellent question — and here's the quick-and-dirty answer. RIM needs a delivery system — a communication medium, as it were — for its technology to work. Not in a position to come up with such a delivery system all by its lonesome, RIM partnered (and built alliances across the globe) with what developed into its network service providers — the usual suspects (meaning the big cellphone companies). These middlemen support the wireless network for your BlackBerry Storm so you can connect to the BlackBerry Internet service — and get all those wonderful e-mails (and spend so much valuable time surfing the Internet). See Figure 1-1 for an overview of this process.

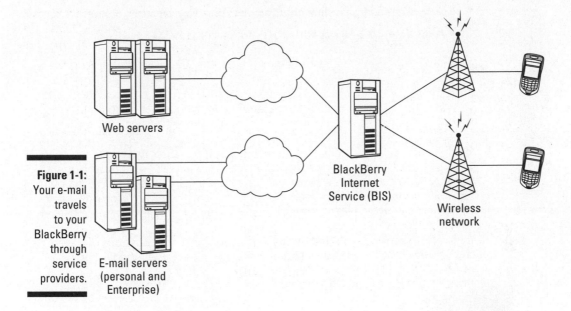

Figure 1-1:
Your e-mail
travels
to your
BlackBerry
through
service
providers.

Web servers

E-mail servers
(personal and
Enterprise)

BlackBerry
Internet
Service (BIS)

Wireless
network

Network service providers don't build alliances for nothing, right? In return, RIM gave them the right to brand their names on the BlackBerry they offer for sale. For example, a T-Mobile BlackBerry looks different from a similar model you get from Vodafone.

Which leads to another question: Do BlackBerry functionalities differ from phone model to phone model? Quick answer: On the core BlackBerry applications (such as Tasks and Contracts), you find no major differences. Other features, such as Instant Messaging, might or might not be supported by the network service provider.

Just to keep the score card straight, when we talk about features available from one network service provider that aren't available from others, we point that out.

Connecting to your computer

Nowadays, a personal computer is a household necessity. People spend so much time on them, and so much information is stored in them. No surprise that BlackBerry works hand-in-hand with your PC. The USB cable that comes with your BlackBerry does more than just charge your device.

Know your BlackBerry history

Your BlackBerry Storm is truly a wondrous thing, boasting many features beyond your ordinary mobile phone. And its "sudden" popularity didn't happen overnight. Like any other good product, BlackBerry Storm has come a long way from its (relatively humble) beginnings.

In the days when the PalmPilot ruled the PDA world, Research In Motion (RIM, the maker of the BlackBerry) was busy in its lab, ignoring the then-popular graffiti input method, and designing a device with a QWERTY keyboard — the kind of keyboard people were already used to from working on their computers. RIM didn't stop there, however. It added an always-connected e-mail capability, making this device a must-have among government officials as well as finance and health professionals.

To meet the needs of government officials and industry professionals, RIM made reliability, security, and durability the priorities when manufacturing its devices. Today, BlackBerry Storm comes from the same line of RIM family products, inheriting all the good genes while boosting usability and adding more functions to its core BlackBerry applications. As a result, BlackBerry is popular among not only *prosumers* (professional customers) but also consumers. Starting with BlackBerry Pearl, RIM has been targeting the mainstream consumer market. Clearly, with BlackBerry Storm, RIM is winning the hearts of consumers while maintaining its hold on the enterprise market.

Part IV helps you use your PC connection with the help of BlackBerry Desktop Manager and all the utilities that come with it. For instance, Chapter 17 talks about installing new applications to your BlackBerry with the help of your PC. In Chapter 14, you find how to sync your device with the Personal Information Manager data that you keep in your PC. You can also read Chapter 15 for directions for switching from another device (even a non-BlackBerry device) to a new BlackBerry. For example, you find out how to import your contact list into your new BlackBerry. Last, Chapter 16 tells you how to protect your data.

If you have a Mac instead of a PC, you can still sync with the PocketMac Sync on your Mac. Research In Motion doesn't actually support the application but does provide the software for free.

Oh, the Things You Can Do!

In the BlackBerry world, it used to be that always-connected e-mail was the primary factor that made BlackBerry very attractive and is likely first in the long list of reasons you got yours.

With Storm you get that, but the touch screen is the center of all attention these days. The touch screen on Storm is just a work of art (and science) and truly a beautiful part of the device. Just hop off your flight, turn on your BlackBerry, and *voilà:* You can receive and send e-mails whether you're in Hong Kong, London, or Paris. Your significant other can get in touch with you wherever you are — just to say hi or to remind you that you promised Aunt Edna a case of Chanel No. 5.

Although e-mail is BlackBerry's strength, that's not the only thing it can do. This section goes beyond e-mail to point out some of the device's other major benefits.

All-in-one multimedia center

Previously, many people hesitated to buy a BlackBerry due to the lack of multimedia functions. They wanted a camera and audio and full video play-back. BlackBerry Storm has changed all that and has more features than you may expect. Not only does Storm have a high-resolution camera — 3.2 megapixels to be exact — but it also has a memory slot for a microSD chip (see Chapter 2). What does that mean?

Well, it means your BlackBerry can function as the following:

- A music and video player that support all the common file formats
- A portable flash drive
- Your personal photo collection

On top of all that, Storm offers a touch screen virtual QWERTY keyboard.

Internet at your fingertips

Yup, with the new BlackBerry Web browser on Storm, you can surf the Net nearly as smoothly as you do a desktop computer. Even better, you can continue chatting with your friends through Instant Messenger, just as if you never left your office. You'll get an alert when your stock is tanking. True, that isn't fun, but you want this information as fast as possible.

Intrigued? Read how Storm can take full advantage of the Web in Chapter 9.

Me and my great personal assistant

You might be saying, "But I'm really a busy person, and I don't have time to browse the Web. What I *do* need is an assistant to help me better organize my day-to-day tasks." If you can afford one, by all means go ahead and hire a personal assistant. The next best thing is a personal *digital* assistant (PDA). Just like people come in many flavors, so do many PDAs.

Whip out that BlackBerry of yours and take a closer look. That's right, your BlackBerry is also a full-fledged PDA, helping you do all this and much more:

- Remember all your acquaintances (see Chapter 4)
- Manage your appointments (Chapter 5)
- Keep a to-do list (Chapter 6)

A touch-screen PC in the palm of your hand

Touch screen? Check.

Remarkable communication device? Check.

Full-fledged PDA? Check.

These capabilities are just the tip of the iceberg. Don't underestimate the device because of its size: Your Storm is also a powerful computer.

Need convincing? Here goes. Out of the box, with no fiddling, it comes with a great set of organizational and productivity tools in the form of programs. Software developers aside from RIM are taking advantage of this growing market — which means hundreds of applications are out there for you. For example, you can download graphic-intensive games or a mortgage calculator.

Download? Absolutely! BlackBerry Storm supports the downloading of applications through BlackBerry Browser. And of course, downloading can be done both wired and wireless (or OTA – over the air). See Chapter 9.

To be honest, we've no way to foresee how many applications will be on the market when you're reading this book. And the price of an application varies, depending on how sophisticated the program is, so we can't really give firm numbers. But if you're curious, check out Chapter 17 and The Part of Tens, where we describe some of the best business applications. You should be able to find some treasures suited to your field of work.

Look Dad, no hands!

Your Storm is equipped with an earphone that doubles as a mic for hands-free talking. This accessory is your doctor's prescription for preventing the stiff neck that comes from wedging your Storm against your ear with your shoulder. At the minimum, it helps free your hands so you can eat Chinese takeout. Some places require you by law to use an earphone while driving (but only when you're talking on a cellphone, of course).

We don't recommend using your cellphone while driving, hands free or not.

But RIM didn't stop with just your standard wired earphones. BlackBerry also supports cool wireless earphones based on Bluetooth technology. How could a bizarrely colored tooth help you here? *Bluetooth* is the name for a (very) short-distance wireless technology that connects devices. See Chapter 11 for how to connect your BlackBerry to a Bluetooth headset.

Chewing on Hardware

Reliability and quality were probably your main concerns when you decided on BlackBerry Storm. Will the product last? Will it perform like the manufacturer says? Will I regret having bought this item six months down the road?

This section looks at some of the hardware features that make buying the BlackBerry device a wise purchase.

Saving power

Anyone with BlackBerry experience knows it's a highly efficient power consumer.

The addition of a colored, high-resolution touch screen has weakened the power efficiency. Power requirements have increased so much that you need to recharge roughly every two days.

But hey, now you have a GPS on deck! We know frequent recharging is a bit of a hassle. A section in Chapter 3 gives tips on prolonging your battery's life, especially when you're traveling.

Putting a sentry on duty

The virtual world isn't exempt from general human nastiness; in fact, every day a battle is fought between those who are trying to attack a system and those who are trying to protect it.

A computer connected to the Internet faces an extra risk of being cracked by a hacker or infected by a virus. Viruses try to replicate themselves and generally bug you.

Fortunately, security is a BlackBerry strong point. Viruses often come as e-mail attachments. However, BlackBerry supports very few file types out of the box (mostly images and documents). You won't face threats from e-mails with these attachments. And data that you send to or get from the PDA is *encrypted* (coded) to prevent snooping.

Chapter 2

Navigating the BlackBerry

In This Chapter

▶ Checking out the features of your BlackBerry

▶ Finding out how to type with your BlackBerry keyboards

You might have heard that BlackBerry Storm is different. From the outside, BlackBerry Storm has been completely revamped. Not only is it sleek and slim, it has a brighter, bigger, and higher-resolution screen than the older models. But what makes it fundamentally different? It has a *touch screen*.

What? No more trackball? No more QWERTY keyboard? How do you select and scroll with the touch screen? What can you do with it? We answer those questions in this chapter. Bear with us and you will be master of your BlackBerry Storm in no time.

Exploring Your BlackBerry's Face

In this section we show you all the keys and features on your BlackBerry Storm. You can see them in Figure 2-1.

First, read about the major features:

✔ **Touch screen:** The *graphical user interface (GUI)* on your BlackBerry Storm. Lets you point to things using your finger instead of having to type.

✔ **Virtual QWERTY keyboard:** This is available on the Storm while you're typing when you tilt the screen on its side (horizontally). You see all the keys individually as you would on a QWERTY BlackBerry.

✔ **Virtual SureType keyboard:** This keyboard layout shows while you're typing with your Storm in its upright (vertical) position. Each virtual SureType key contains two letters.

Left convenience key

Lock key

Notification LED

Mute key

Figure 2-1:
The main
BlackBerry
Storm
features
are here,
including
a popular
e-mail/SMS
alert
program
called
PeeKaWho.

Menu key

Send key

Find key

Escape key

Touch screen

Right convenience key

TIP

✓ **Escape key:** This key cancels a selection or returns you to a previous page in an application. If you hold it down, escape takes you to the Home screen from any program.

✓ **Menu key:** This key displays the full menu of the application you're using.

✓ **Convenience keys:** Your BlackBerry Storm has two convenience keys. By default, the convenience keys are preprogrammed to open an application. In Chapter 3, we show you how to reprogram the convenience keys to display the programs you use the most.

- ✔ **microSD slot:** You can access the microSD slot by removing the back cover, but without removing the battery. The microSD slot is a crucial element to your BlackBerry media experience.

- ✔ **Send key:** This key takes you straight to the Phone application, regardless of which application you're currently using. If you're already in the Phone application, the send key starts dialing the number you entered.

- ✔ **End key:** Use this key to end your call. If not on a phone call, this key allows you to jump straight back to the Home screen from wherever you are.

- ✔ **Power key:** Press and hold the Power key to turn your BlackBerry on or off. Or you can do press and hold the Turn Power Off icon.

- ✔ **Mute key:** Mutes a call when on a call.

- ✔ **Lock key:** Quickly locks the BlackBerry screen. You'd use this when you want to put your BlackBerry in your pocket and prevent accidental typing, for instance.

Using the Touch Screen

When you first turn on your BlackBerry, the display screen displays the *Home screen,* which is your introduction to your BlackBerry Storm's GUI. The different icons represent the different applications in your BlackBerry.

If you tilt your BlackBerry sideways, the screen follows you.

We use these terms to show you how to interact with your BlackBerry Storm.

- ✔ **Tap** is a light touch. It allows you to highlight a choice in a list or place the typing cursor in a particular place. Tapping does not, however, select or confirm a choice.

- ✔ **Touch-press** by firmly touching and pressing on something to select it.

- ✔ **Finger scroll** by keeping your finger on the touch screen and moving up, down, left, or right on the screen. You scroll to different parts of the screen.

Applications have a row of icons on the bottom of the screen. You can access these shortcuts without using the menu key. If this is your first touch-screen device, play and have fun with it. Trust us; it won't bite.

Tapping the Keyboards: QWERTY and SureType

Surprised? Just when you thought the term QWERTY wasn't going to be part of this book, it is. That's right. In the following sections, we talk about the onscreen — or virtual — keyboards that you use to enter information.

Virtual QWERTY keyboard

You see the virtual QWERTY keyboard appear if you tilt your BlackBerry Storm sideways while entering text into a text field. See Figure 2-2.

Figure 2-2: This BlackBerry Storm displays its virtual QWERTY keyboard.

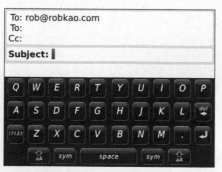

You can hide the virtual keyboard by pressing the menu key and touch-pressing Hide Keyboard.

Whether you use your pinky or your index finger, how you type on your BlackBerry is up to you. However, most people find that typing with two thumbs is the most efficient way to type on a BlackBerry Storm. And like the SureType keyboard with its Custom Dictionary, the QWERTY keyboard helps you as you type so you can get the word out (literally) with less keystrokes.

Virtual SureType keyboard

The SureType keyboard appears when you hold your BlackBerry Storm upright (vertical). Many keys share letters, as shown in Figure 2-3. The idea is that SureType is smart enough to figure out what letter you want. Basically, you can type with only one thumb, and your BlackBerry learns the words that you frequently use.

For example, if you want to type the word *hi,* press the GH key and then the UI key. SureType lists the words it thinks you're typing, as shown in Figure 2-3. If the first word is what you want, simply touch the word onscreen or the virtual Space key. The word is selected and you can keep typing. If what you want appears a little later in the list, finger scroll to the word and touch it.

Figure 2-3:
Did you
want to type
Hi or gi?

These tips can speed up your SureType learning curve:

- ✓ **Always finish typing a word before correcting it.** This way, SureType learns what you want to type next time.

- ✓ **If SureType correctly gets the word you're typing (on the first try), use the Space key to move on.**

- ✓ **Take advantage of Custom Dictionary, which is a list of words that you define.** More on this later in this section.

- ✓ **Type! Type! Type!** Because SureType learns how you type, the more you use it, the faster it adapts.

Multitap

Besides SureType, you can type in another mode while BlackBerry is upright: *multitap.*

The best way to explain multitap is by example. Say you want to type an h character on the virtual SureType keyboard. You search out the h on your keyboard but notice the key reads GH. What's a person to do? Do you really want to go through life writing *GHello* for *Hello*?

Your problem has a perfectly easy solution. To get the letter g, tap the GH key once. To get the letter h — the second letter on the key — tap the key twice — hence the term *multitap.*

Custom Dictionary

SureType keeps all its learned words in a safe place — a *Wordlist,* to be precise. You can review your SureType Wordlist — and even add to it — using the Custom Dictionary option.

Using the Custom Dictionary option to add words or proper names to the list means that SureType doesn't have to learn them when you're actually typing.

To see or add words by using the Custom Wordlist option, follow these steps:

1. **From the Home screen, press the menu key and then touch-press the options icon.**

2. **Select Custom Dictionary.**

   The Custom Dictionary opens, where all the words that SureType has learned are listed. (If you purchased your BlackBerry recently, there might be only a few words or even no words in this list, depending on how often you've used SureType mode to type.)

3. **Press the menu key and then touch-press New.**

4. **To save your changes, press the menu key and then touch-press Save.**

Getting people's names right is tough with SureType, but thankfully you can make sure that SureType automatically learns all the names in Contacts as follows:

1. **From the Home screen, press the menu key and then touch-press the options icon.**

2. **Touch-press Localization.**

   The Localization option screen appears, where the handy Input Option button makes its home.

3. **Touch-press the Input Option button.**

   The Fast Options screen displays with the following options:

   - *Auto Word Learning:* If turned on, SureType learns as you type.
   - *Use Address Book as Data Source:* If turned on, SureType learns all the names in your Contacts.

4. **Make sure the Use Address Book as Data Source option is turned on.**

   If it isn't, touch-press On from the drop-down list.

5. **To save your changes, press the menu key and then touch-press Save.**

Physical Keys and More

Although most of the key entry on the Storm is done through the onscreen keyboards (see the "Tapping the Keyboards: QWERTY and SureType" section), there are a few physical keys to help you navigate the user interface of your Storm quicker.

Escape key

Simple yet useful, the escape key allows you to return to a previous screen or cancel a selection. The escape key is the arrow key to the left of the End Key.

Menu key (BlackBerry key)

The menu key brings up the full menu for the application you are using. When you're on the Home screen, pressing the menu key displays a list of applications installed on your BlackBerry. If you want to change the order of the applications in the list, see Chapter 3.

Convenience keys

Your BlackBerry Storm has two convenience keys, one on the left and one on the right. By default, the right convenience key opens the Camera and the left convenience key opens the voice command application. Think of these two keys as shortcuts to the application you need fast access to. You can program and change these keys to open whatever is installed on your BlackBerry; see Chapter 3 for more info.

microSD slot

Your BlackBerry Storm comes with tons of internal memory: 1GB to be exact. If you're a music or video fan, you know that 1GB isn't enough to hold anything entertaining. But no need to worry. The folks at Research In Motion incorporated a microSD (external memory card) slot into your BlackBerry Storm so you can add memory and store all the media files you want in your BlackBerry Storm.

You can purchase a microSD card separately for a relatively low price these days. At the time of this writing, a 4GB microSD card costs $20.

Switching applications

When you are moving around in an application (such as Browser), an option called Switch Application appears when you press the menu key. Switch Application, which is similar to Alt+Tab under Windows, lets you multitask between applications; see Figure 2-4.

Figure 2-4:
Switch
application
menu.

If you always use a particular application, such as Tasks, you can program the convenience key so you can get to your favorite application even more quickly than by using the Switch Application function.

Chapter 3

Whipping Up a Storm of Your Own

*Y*ou want to have your BlackBerry around as long as you possibly can. (Or, at least until you have the bucks for that way-cool new model that's coming down the pike.) And, for the time that you *do* have your device, you'll want to trick it out. (C'mon, admit it — your BlackBerry is definitely a fashion statement.)

In addition to customizing, you want to keep your BlackBerry in tip-top shape by watching out for things such as battery life and information security. Luckily for you, this chapter fills you in on all you need to know to keep your BlackBerry Storm a finely tuned (and yet quirkily personal) little SmartPhone.

Making Your BlackBerry Yours

BlackBerry devices are increasingly popular — so much so that close to 20 million BlackBerrys are out there serving the needs of people like you. Because of this fact, we're certain that finding ways to distinguish your BlackBerry from your colleagues' is high on your list of priorities.

Your wish is our command. Follow the tips and techniques outlined in this section and you, too, can personalize to your heart's content.

Branding your BlackBerry

Like any number of other electronic gadgets that you could possibly own, your BlackBerry comes to you with a collection of settings. This section helps you put your name on your BlackBerry, both figuratively and literally.

You can start by branding your name on your BlackBerry:

1. **Press the menu key and touch-press the options icon.**

2. **Touch-press Owner options.**

   You see places to enter your owner information.

3. **Enter your name in the Name field and your contact information in the Information field.**

   Phrase a message that would make sense to any possible Good Samaritan who might find your lost BlackBerry and want to get it back to you.

   If you lock or don't use your BlackBerry for a while, the standby screen displays the owner information that you entered. Read how to lock your BlackBerry, either manually or by using an auto setting, as described in the later section, "Keeping Your BlackBerry Safe."

4. **Press the menu key and touch-press Save.**

Choose a language, any language

Set the language to your native tongue so you don't need to hire a translator to use your BlackBerry. You can also set your input method of choice here, which can affect whether AutoText shows up. Don't worry. We explain what that means in the next section.

Here's how you choose a language:

1. **Press the menu key and touch-press the options icon.**

2. **Touch-press Localization (or Language) option.**

   Here you can choose the language and input method.

3. **Touch-press the Language field and then select your native (or preferred) tongue.**

   Language choices vary depending on your network provider and region (North America, Europe, and so on). Most handhelds sold in North America default to English or English (United States).

   If your network provider supports it, you can install more languages into your BlackBerry by using Application Loader in BlackBerry Desktop Manager. For more information on Application Loader, see Chapter 17.

4. **Press the menu key and touch-press Save.**

   Isn't it great when you can actually read what's on the screen? But don't think that you're finished quite yet. You still have some personalizing to do.

Typing with ease using AutoText

Even the most devoted BlackBerry user has to admit that typing on a full keyboard is easier than thumb typing on a BlackBerry. To even the score a bit, your BlackBerry Storm comes with an AutoText feature, which is a kind of shorthand.

AutoText basically works with a pool of abbreviations that you set up. Then you type an abbreviation to get the word you associated with that abbreviation. For example, after setting up *b/c* as an AutoText word for *because,* anytime you type b/c, you automatically get *because* onscreen.

The whole AutoText thing works only if you set up your own personal code, mapping your abbreviations to their meanings. (This is why we're discussing AutoText as part of our personalization discussion.)

To set up your own code, do the following:

1. **Press the menu key and touch-press the options icon.**

2. **Touch-press AutoText option.**

   You can choose to see (or search for) existing AutoText words or create new ones.

3. **Press the menu key and touch-press New.**

   The AutoText screen appears, as shown in Figure 3-1.

Figure 3-1:
Create
AutoText
here.

4. **In the Replace field, enter the characters that you want to replace.**

5. **In the With field, type what replaces your characters.**

6. **Choose between two options in the Using field:**

   • *SmartCase* capitalizes the first letter when the context calls for that, such as the first word in a sentence.

- *Specified Case* replaces your AutoText with the exact text found in the With field.

TIP

For example, say you have the AutoText *bbg* set up for the term *blackberryGoodies.com,* and you want it to appear as is, in terms of letter cases (the first *b* is lowercase). If you choose SmartCase for this AutoText entry, and it's the first word in a sentence, the word is capitalized; that isn't what you want. On the other hand, if you use Specified Case, your AutoText always appears as *blackberryGoodies.com* no matter where it is in the sentence.

7. **Scroll to the Language field and touch-press All Locales.**

   We prefer All Locales because regardless of the language input method (for example, French), any self-created AutoText is available for you to use. In the case of the AutoText *bbg* (*blackberryGoodies.com*), you can use this AutoText whether you're typing in French or Chinese. On the other hand, if you select only the French input method for *bbg* as the Language field, you could use this only if your input method is set to French in the Language option.

   You can choose the input method of your choice in the Language options. We go over choosing a language input method next.

8. **Press the menu key and touch-press Save.**

TIP

If you specify a language input method other than All Locales, your input method setting in the Language option must match the Language field in AutoText to use your newly created AutoText:

1. **Press the menu key and touch-press the options icon.**

2. **Touch-press Localization (or Language) option.**

   Here you can choose the language and input method.

3. **Select the Input Method field and then select the input method you need from the list.**

   For your new AutoText setting to work (assuming that you didn't choose All Locales as the language for your AutoText), this option needs to match the input method set in your Language option.

4. **Press the menu key and touch-press Save.**

Inserting text shortcuts

If you frequently give out your BlackBerry phone number or PIN in e-mails, you'll appreciate what we call text shortcuts. Basically, you can use the AutoText feature to add a customized word for preset items — things such as your BlackBerry number, PIN, or just the date — so you don't have to type them all the time.

Keep in mind that we're talking about your BlackBerry PIN here — your device's unique identifying number — and not the PIN someone would use to empty out your checking account with the help of one of those automated tellers. For more on BlackBerry PINs, see Chapter 8.

To add a text shortcut for your phone number, for example, follow these steps:

1. **Bring up the AutoText screen.**

   AutoText is an option in Options.

2. **Type an appropriate word in the Replace field.**

   mynum would work nicely.

3. **Touch-press the With field and type** "my number is.

4. **Press the menu key and choose Insert Macro.**

   You're prompted with a pop-up to select from a list of preset items.

5. **Select the Phone Number (%p) option.**

6. **Press the menu key and touch-press Save.**

7. **Test your AutoText by drafting a simple e-mail and type** mynum.

Customizing your screen's look and feel

You can get the display font, font size, and screen contrast to your liking. Now we know that some of you don't give a hoot if your fonts are Batang or Bookman as long as you can read the text, but we also know that some of you won't stop configuring the fonts until you get them absolutely right.

For all you tweakers out there, here's how you play around with your BlackBerry's fonts:

1. **Press the menu key and touch-press the options icon.**

2. **Touch-press Screen/Keyboard.**

   The Screen/Keyboard screen appears with various customizable fields, as shown in Figure 3-2.

3. **Touch-press the Font Family field and then touch-press a font from the drop-down list.**

4. **Continuing down the Screen/Keyboard screen, touch-press the Font Size field, and then touch-press a font size.**

   The smaller the font size, the more you can see onscreen; however, a small font is harder on the eyes.

Note: As you finger scroll up and down the list of fonts and font sizes, notice that the text "The quick brown fox jumps over the lazy dog" in the background takes on the look of the selected font and size so that you can preview what the particular text looks like.

Figure 3-2:
The Screen/
Keyboard
screen is
waiting for
personaliza-
tion.

  5. Press the menu key and touch-press Save.

Similar to setting font size, you can also play with font style to set it to bold, italic, or neither. At this point, you're probably wondering what Antialias Mode is for. Think of antialias as a way your BlackBerry renders alphabet characters. With No Antialiasing set, your fonts have round edges. With Antialiasing set, your fonts have sharp edges. The difference between the two settings is subtle.

With fonts out of the way, it's time to change the brightness of your screen as well as a few other viewing options, including how to program the convenience keys so every time you press it, the convenience key opens the application that you use most often:

  1. Press the menu key and touch-press the options icon.

  2. Touch-press Screen/Keyboard.

  3. Touch-press the Backlight Brightness field and then select the desired brightness from the drop-down list.

  You can choose from 10 to 100, where 10 is the darkest and 100 is the brightest.

4. **Touch-press the Convenience Key Opens field.**

5. **Touch-press an application that you want the convenience key to open.**

   Typically, we like to set these keys to open applications that we often need, like the Browser application or the Task application.

6. **Touch-press the Backlight Timeout field and choose an amount of time.**

   You can choose from ten seconds up to two minutes. The lower this setting, the less time you'll have backlighting (after you press each key). However, a low setting helps you conserve battery life.

7. **Touch-press the Tap Interval field and decide how sensitive you want the tap to be.**

   You can choose from 100 to 500, where 100 is the most sensitive and 500 is the least sensitive.

8. **Touch-press the Hover Period field and decide how sensitive you want your touch on the touch screen to be.**

   Here, 100 is the most sensitive and 1000 is the least sensitive. Keep in mind that if your setting is too sensitive, it might be hard to control.

   When you hover your finger over an icon or link without touch-pressing the screen, a small yellow text box appears giving you hints at what you can expect by touch-pressing the icon.

9. **To confirm your changes, press the menu key and touch-press Save.**

Choosing themes

Your BlackBerry is preloaded with different *themes,* which are predefined sets of looks (wallpaper, fonts, menu layout) for your BlackBerry. You can download themes from BlackBerry's mobile Web site.

Regardless of what BlackBerry model you have, follow these steps to change your theme:

1. **Press the menu key and touch-press the options icon.**

2. **Touch-press the Theme option.**

   You see a list of available themes; your Storm may come with only one theme, but you can always download more.

3. **Touch-press the theme you want.**

4. **Press the menu key and touch-press Activate.**

   You see the change after a short wait.

You can download other themes. Just remember that you have to use your BlackBerry, not your PC, to access the following URLs:

- http://mobile.blackberry.com
- http://blackberrywallpaper.com

Wallpapering

Like your desktop PC, you can customize the BlackBerry Home screen with personalized *wallpaper*.

You set an image to be your BlackBerry Home screen background by using the BlackBerry Media application:

1. **From the Home screen, press the menu key and touch-press the Media application.**

    The Media application opens, where you see different categories: Music, Video, Ring tones, and Pictures.

2. **Touch-press the Picture category.**

    Doing so brings up three lines:

    - *All Pictures* shows you a thumbnail view of all your photos — the ones you took and the ones that came with your BlackBerry Storm.

    - *Picture Folders* lists the folders that contain photos, as well as a thumbnail list of the photos.

    - *Sample Pictures* shows you a thumbnail view of the pictures that came with your BlackBerry Storm.

3. **Touch-press All Pictures.**

4. **Touch-press the picture you want to use for your Home screen wallpaper.**

    The selected picture appears in full-screen view.

5. **Press the menu key and touch-press Set as Home Screen Image.**

    The picture is now your new Home screen wallpaper.

6. **Press and hold the escape key to return to the Home screen and see the result.**

    If you hold your BlackBerry Storm in its upright (vertical) position, you see your new wallpaper.

You can download free wallpaper here as long as you use your BlackBerry, not your PC, to access the URLs:

🖊 http://mobile.blackberry.com

🖊 blackberrywallpapers.com

After you have your BlackBerry's look and feel just the way you want, do one more thing before you move on: Get your BlackBerry sounding the way you want it to.

Ringing freedom

The whole appeal of the BlackBerry phenomenon is the idea that this little electronic device can make your life easier. One of the ways it accomplishes this is by acting as your personal reminder service — letting you know when an appointment is coming up, a phone call is coming in, an e-mail has arrived, and so on. Basically, your BlackBerry is set to bark at you if it knows something it thinks you should know too. Figure 3-3 lists the kinds of things your BlackBerry considers bark-worthy, ranging from Browser alerts to Tasks deadlines.

Figure 3-3:
Set
attention-
needy
applications
here.

Different people react differently to different sounds. Some BlackBerry barks would be greatly appreciated by certain segments of the population, whereas other segments might react to the same sound by pitching their BlackBerry under the nearest bus. The folks at Research In Motion are well aware of this fact and have devised a great way for you to customize how you want your BlackBerry to bark at you — they call it your *profile*.

You can jump right into things by using a predefined profile.

Checking out the different profiles

Each profile is divided into seven categories that represent the application for which you can define alerts:

- **Browser:** Alerts you when you receive a new channel *push,* which is a Web page sent to your BlackBerry as an icon on your Home screen.

- **Calendar:** Alerts you when you have upcoming appointments.

- **Level1 Messages (urgent e-mail messages):** Alerts you with a special tone when you have an urgent e-mail (e-mail with an important or priority flag). Also, a BlackBerry PIN-to-PIN message can be considered urgent. For more on PIN-to-PIN, see Chapter 8.

- **Messages:** Alerts you when a new e-mail message is in your inbox.

- **Phone:** Alerts you if there is an incoming call or a new voice mail.

- **SMS:** Alerts you when you have an SMS message.

- **Tasks:** Alerts you of an upcoming to-do deadline.

You can personalize the alert on all the listed applications. Because the way you customize them is similar, we use one application (Messages) as an example in the text that follows, as we customize a predefined profile that comes with your BlackBerry.

Customizing a predefined profile

If you're okay with customizing a predefined, factory-loaded profile, just do the following:

1. **From the BlackBerry Home screen, touch-press the Profile application.**

   A screen lists different profiles: Quiet, Vibrate, Normal. See Figure 3-4.

2. **Touch-press Set Ring Tones/Alerts.**

   A screen lists different applications. Note that you are setting the ring tones/alerts for whatever profile that is currently in selection. For example, if you're currently using Normal, when you touch-press Set Ring Tones/Alerts, you are modifying the Normal profile's setting.

3. **Touch-press the Message [Email] application.**

   If you have multiple e-mail accounts routed to your BlackBerry, you can set settings for each.

4. **Touch-press the Ring Tone field and then touch-press a tune from the drop-down list.**

   Doing so enables sound when e-mail arrives for this e-mail account. If you want any sounds to play, you can choose this in the Volume field.

Figure 3-4:
A Profile
application
helps you
personalize.

5. **Touch-press the Volume field and then touch-press to select the volume level you desire.**

   You can choose from silent to 10 for loudest.

6. **Touch-press the Vibration field and then touch-press Custom.**

   This brings out more options for vibration. You can control

   • How many vibrations each e-mail triggers

   • Vibration duration

   • Whether you want the vibration to happen when your Storm is in its holster

7. **Press the menu key and touch-press Save.**

   As mentioned, you can do the same to personalize other applications listed in each profile.

 Maybe you get a lot of e-mail. You probably don't want your BlackBerry sounding off 200 times a day. Set your BlackBerry Storm to notify you only if an e-mail is marked urgent, requiring your immediate attention. Set the notification for your Messages application to None for both In Holster and Out of Holster. Then in the Level1 option, set notification for both In Holster and Out of Holster.

Keeping Your BlackBerry Safe

The folks at Research In Motion take security seriously, and so should you. Always set up a password on your BlackBerry. If your BlackBerry hasn't prompted you to set up a password, you should immediately do so.

Here's how it's done:

1. **From the BlackBerry Home screen, touch-press the options icon.**

2. **Touch-press Password.**

3. **Touch-press Disable Settings and select Enabled.**

4. **Touch-press Security Timeout and select a time.**

   Choose anywhere from 1 minute up to 1 hour.

5. **Press the menu key and touch-press Save.**

   You're prompted for a password.

6. **Type a password, and then type it again for verification.**

   From this point on, whenever you lock your BlackBerry and want to use it again, you have to type the password. If you don't use your BlackBerry, it locks according to Security Timeout setting.

Setting up your password is a good first step, but just having a password won't help much if you don't take the further step of locking your BlackBerry when you're not using it. (You don't want people at the office or sitting at the next table at the coffee shop checking out your e-mails or phone history when you take a bathroom break, do you?) How do you lock your BlackBerry? Press the menu key, and then touch-press the Lock icon on the Home screen.

Part II
Getting Organized with Your Storm

The 5th Wave — By Rich Tennant

BUS STOP

"Well, here's what happened–I forgot to put 'dressing' on my 'To Do' list."

In this part . . .

This part covers how to use your BlackBerry Storm to its fullest to get you — and keep you — organized. Peruse the chapters here to find out how to use your Contacts applications, keep appointments, keep on track with to-do lists, do arithmetic calculations, and make notes.

Chapter 4

Remembering and Locating Your Acquaintances

In This Chapter

▶ Adding, viewing, editing, and deleting contacts

▶ Finding a contact in Contacts

▶ Organizing Contacts

▶ Sharing BlackBerry Storm's contacts

▶ Transferring contacts to your BlackBerry Storm

Address books were around long before the BlackBerry was conceived. Your BlackBerry Storm Contacts serves the same function as any other: to record and organize information about people. It also gives you a central place to reach your contacts by landline phone, cellphone, e-mail, or the speedy messaging of PIN, SMS, MMS, or BlackBerry Messenger.

You can benefit from using your BlackBerry Contacts if any of the following fit you and your lifestyle:

✔ You travel.

✔ You meet clients frequently.

✔ You spend a lot of time on the phone.

✔ You ask people for their phone number or e-mail address more than once.

✔ You carry around a paper day planner.

✔ Your wallet is full of important business cards, with phone numbers written on the backs, that you can never find.

If you're one of those stubborn folks who insist they don't need an address book — "I'm doing just fine without one, thank you very much!" — think of it this way: You've been using a virtual address book all the time — the one buried in your cellphone. And that address book often isn't even a very good one! Read this chapter to see how to transfer all that good contact info from an old phone into your new BlackBerry-based Contacts.

Accessing Your Contacts

The Contacts icon looks like an old-fashioned address book. (Remember those?) If you have a hard time locating it, Figure 4-1 shows what it looks like. Opening Contacts couldn't be simpler: Just touch-press the Contacts icon.

Figure 4-1:
The
Contacts
icon.

You can access Contacts from Phone, Messages, BlackBerry Messenger, and Calendar. For example, say you're in Calendar and you want to invite people to one of your meetings. Look no further — Contacts is in the menu, ready to lend a helping hand.

Cleaning Your Contacts

Getting a new gizmo is always exciting; your new toy is full of features you're dying to try out. Calling someone was probably the first thing you wanted to do with your new BlackBerry Storm. But wait a second. You'll have to type the phone number not just this time, but each time you want to call. What a hassle.

Most people — social creatures that we are — keep a list of contacts somewhere like an e-mail program, an old cellphone, or on a piece of paper (tucked away in a wallet). We're pretty sure you have some kind of list somewhere. The trick is getting that list into your BlackBerry Storm so you can access the info more efficiently. The good news is that getting the information into your BlackBerry Storm isn't hard.

Often the simplest way to get contact information into your BlackBerry Storm is to enter it manually. However, if you've invested a lot of time keeping the information updated on your desktop computer, you might want to hot sync that data into your BlackBerry Storm. For more on synchronizing data, check Chapter 14.

Creating a contact

Imagine you've just run into Jane, an old high-school friend you haven't seen in years. Jane wants to give you her number, but you don't have a pen handy. Are you forced to chant her phone number to yourself until you can scare up a writing implement? Not if you have your handy BlackBerry Storm on you.

With BlackBerry Storm in hand, follow these steps to create a new contact:

1. **On the Home screen, touch-press the Contacts icon.**

   Contacts opens. You can also access Contacts from different applications. For example, check Chapter 7 on how to access Contacts from Messages.

2. **Touch-press the plus icon located in the bottom of the screen.**

   The New Contact screen appears, as shown in Figure 4-2.

Figure 4-2:
Create a
new contact
here.

3. **Enter the contact information in the appropriate fields.**

Use your BlackBerry Storm virtual keyboard to enter contact information. Hold the device sideways (landscape) to get the full QWERTY keyboard. When entering an e-mail address, press the Space key to insert an *at* symbol (@) or a period (.).

We don't think you can overdo it when entering a person's contact information. Enter as much info as you possibly can. Maybe the benefit won't be obvious now, but when your memory fails or your boss needs a critical piece of data that you happen to have, you'll thank us for this advice.

To create another new, blank e-mail field for the same contact, press the menu key and touch-press Add Email Address. You can have up to three e-mail addresses per contact.

BlackBerry Storm can dial an extension after the initial phone number. When entering the phone number, type the primary phone number, touch-press P on the virtual keyboard, and add the extension number.

4. **Press the menu key.**

5. **Touch-press Save.**

Jane is added to the list, as shown in Figure 4-3.

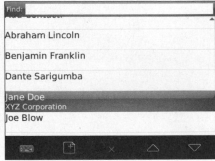

Figure 4-3: The Contacts screen shows your new contact.

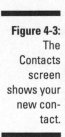

The menu is always available through the menu key. The application is smart enough to figure out which items are more relevant based on what you're doing. You can always touch-press the full menu listing.

Taking notes

The Notes field in the New Address screen (you might need to scroll down a bit to see it) is useful for adding a unique description about your contact. For example, use the field to jog your memory with tidbits such as *Knows somebody at ABC Corporation* or *Can provide introduction to a Broadway agent.* Or perhaps your note is something personal, such as *Likes golf; has 2 children: boy, 7 & girl, 3; husband's name is Ray.* It's up to you. Again, the more useful the information, the better it serves you.

Adding your own fields

Perhaps your contact information doesn't fit into any of the available fields. Although you can't create fields from scratch, you can commandeer one of the User fields for your own purposes.

The User fields are at the bottom of the screen; you have to scroll down to see them. Use these fields any way you want; you can even change the field's name. For example, you can rename User fields to capture suffixes (such as MD, PhD, and so on). Or how about these tidbits:

- ✔ Profession
- ✔ Hobbies
- ✔ School
- ✔ Nickname

Keep in mind that changing the Users field name for a particular contact changes it for *all* your contacts.

Follow along to rename a User field:

1. **While editing a contact, scroll to the bottom of the screen to navigate to one of the User fields.**

2. **Press the menu key.**

3. **Touch-press Change Field Name.**

   Note: The Change Field Name selection on the menu appears only if the cursor is in a User field.

4. **Use the virtual keyboard to type the new name.**

5. **Touch-press the enter key.**

6. **Press the menu key.**

7. **Touch-press Save.**

   You're all set.

Adding a picture to a contact

Most phones can display a picture of whoever's calling; BlackBerry Storm is no stranger to this neat feature.

1. **Have a picture of the person.**

   See Chapter 11 for more about taking photos with your BlackBerry Storm.

2. **Get the photo to your BlackBerry Storm.**

You can send it via e-mail, copy it to the microSD card, or copy it to the built-in memory of Storm. If you don't know how to use the microSD, Chapter 12 is your gateway to media satisfaction.

 3. **From the Home screen, touch-press the Contacts icon.**

 4. **Touch-press a contact.**

    The contact is highlighted.

 5. **Press the menu key.**

 6. **Touch-press Edit.**

    The Edit screen appears.

 7. **Press the menu key.**

 8. **Touch-press Add Picture; see Figure 4-4.**

Figure 4-4:
Add a picture here.

 9. **Navigate to the drive and folder that has the picture.**

    You can use multiple locations for storing media files (including pictures). Chapter 12 gives you the scoop.

10. **Touch-press the picture you want.**

    The picture appears on the screen.

11. **Press the menu key.**

12. **Touch-press Crop and Save.**

13. **Press the menu key.**

14. **Touch-press Save.**

Assigning a tone

Oh no, your ringing BlackBerry has woken you. Ring tones help you decide whether to ignore the call or get up. Hopefully, you can easily switch yourself to sleep mode if you ignore the call.

Follow these steps to assign a ring tone to one of your contacts:

1. **While editing a contact, touch-press Phone under the Custom Ring Tones/Alerts portion of the Edit Contact screen (refer to left of Figure 4-5).**

Figure 4-5:
Left: starting place to customize ring tone; right: selecting the ring tone.

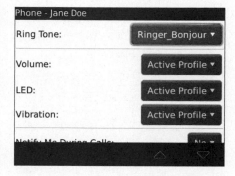

A screen similar to the right of Figure 4-5 gives you an option to customize the ring tone settings. From this screen, you can select which ring tone to use, set the volume, control whether to make the LED blink, make the phone vibrate, and whether the setting works while on a call.

2. **Touch-press the tone settings you want.**

3. **Press the menu key.**

4. **Touch-press Save.**

5. **Press the menu key.**

6. **Touch-press Save.**

Adding contacts from other BlackBerry applications

When you get an e-mail message or a call, that person's contact information is in Messages or Phone. It's just logical to add the information.

You might've noticed that Phone lists only *outgoing numbers.* That's half of what you need. Oddly enough, you can access incoming phone calls in Messages.

1. **Touch-press Messages from Home screen.**

   Messages opens.

2. **Press the menu key.**

   A menu appears.

3. **Touch-press View Folder.**

4. **Touch-press Phone Call Logs.**

A phone log entry stays as long as you have free space in your BlackBerry Storm. When BlackBerry runs out of space (which could take years, depending on how you use it), it deletes read e-mails and phone logs, starting from the oldest.

Creating a contact from an existing e-mail address or phone number in Messages is easy.

1. **Touch-press Messages from Home screen.**

   Messages opens.

2. **Touch-press the e-mail address or the phone number.**

   A menu appears.

3. **Touch-press Add to Contacts.**

   A new New Contact screen appears, filled with that particular piece of information.

4. **Enter the rest of the information you know.**

5. **Press the menu key.**

6. **Touch-press Save.**

This is just one more sign of BlackBerry's ongoing attempt to make your life easier.

Viewing a contact

You just entered your friend's name into your BlackBerry, but you have this nagging thought that you typed the wrong phone number. You want to quickly view the information. Here's how you do it:

1. **On the Home screen, touch-press the Contacts icon.**

   Contacts opens.

2. **Scroll to and touch-press the contact name you want.**

   Touching the name is the same as opening the menu and choosing View — just quicker.

View mode displays only information that's been filled in, as shown in Figure 4-6. It doesn't bother showing fields that have no information.

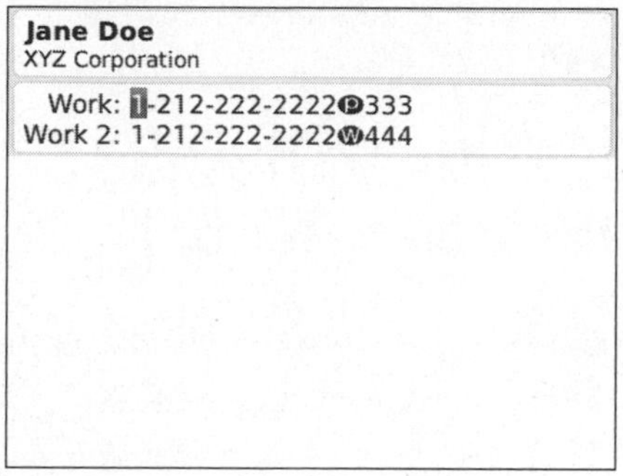

Jane Doe
XYZ Corporation

Work: 1-212-222-2222333
Work 2: 1-212-222-2222 444

Figure 4-6:
View mode
for a
contact.

Editing a contact

Change is an inevitable part of life. If you want to keep current the information you diligently put in your Contacts, you'll have to do some updating now and then.

To update a contact, follow these steps:

1. **On the BlackBerry Storm Home screen, touch-press the Contacts icon.**

   Contacts opens.

2. **Scroll to and highlight a contact name and press the menu key.**

3. **Touch-press Edit.**

   The Edit Contact screen appears.

   In any BlackBerry Storm application, including Contacts, you can display a menu by pressing the menu key. You see the Edit option in the menu right below View.

4. **Edit the contact information as you see fit.**

   Hold the device sideways to get the full QWERTY keyboard.

5. **Press the menu key.**

6. **Touch-press Save.**

   The edit you made for this contact is saved.

When you're editing information and want to totally replace the entry, clear the contents. When you're in an *editable field* (as opposed to a *selectable field*), just press the menu key and touch-press Clear Field. This feature is always available to an editable field.

Deleting a contact

It's time to get rid of somebody's contact information in your Contacts. Maybe it's a case of duplication or a bit of bad blood. Either way, BlackBerry Storm makes it easy to delete a contact.

1. **On the Home screen, touch-press the Contacts icon.**

   Contacts opens.

2. **Scroll to and highlight a contact name you want to delete.**

3. **Touch-press the Delete (x) icon at the bottom of the screen.**

   A confirmation screen appears, as shown in Figure 4-7.

4. **Touch-press Delete.**

   The contact disappears from your contact list.

Figure 4-7:
The con-
firmation
screen
when you're
about to
delete a
contact.

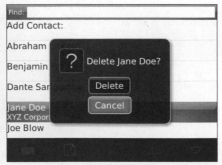

Dealing with the confirmation screen can be a pain if you want to delete several contacts in a row. If you're *100-percent* sure you want to ditch a number of contacts, you can suspend the Confirmation feature by setting the Confirm Delete option to No in the Contacts Options screen. Check the "Setting preferences" section later in this chapter for more on Contacts options.

Copying Contacts from Desktop Applications

Most people use desktop applications to maintain their contacts — you know, Microsoft Outlook, IBM Lotus Notes, or Novell GroupWise. A word to the wise: You don't want to maintain two address books. That's a recipe for disaster. Luckily for you, RIM makes it easy to get your various address books — BlackBerry, desktop, laptop, whatever — in sync.

Your BlackBerry Storm comes with BlackBerry Desktop Manager (BDM), a collection of programs, one of which is Synchronize. Synchronize allows you to synchronize the data between your device and the PC software. It also allows you to set up and configure the behavior of the program, including how the fields in the desktop version of Address Book map to Contacts fields in your BlackBerry.

Check out Chapter 14, which details using the Synchronize feature of BlackBerry Desktop Manager device.

Looking for Someone?

Somehow — usually through typing and shuttling data between devices — you've created a nice long list of contacts in your Contacts. Nice enough, we suppose — but useless unless you can find the phone number of Rufus T. Firefly at the drop of a hat.

That's where the Find screen comes in. In fact, the first thing you see in Contacts when you open it is the Find screen, as shown in Figure 4-8.

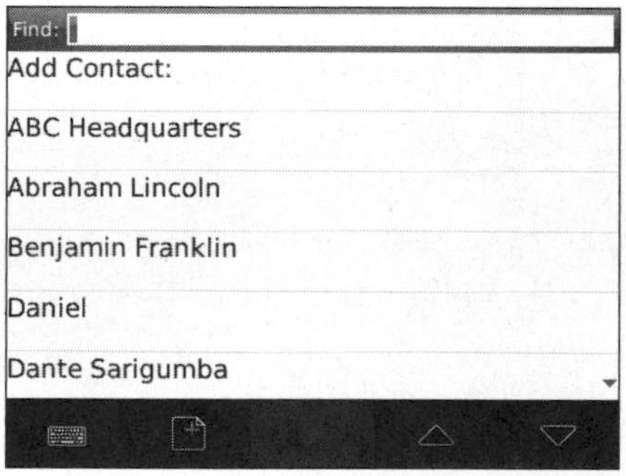

Figure 4-8:
Your search
starts here.

> Find:
> Add Contact:
> ABC Headquarters
> Abraham Lincoln
> Benjamin Franklin
> Daniel
> Dante Sarigumba

You can conveniently search through your contacts by following these steps:

1. **In the Find field, enter the letters that start the name you're searching for.**

   Your search criterion is the person's name. You can enter the last name, first name, or both. The list is usually sorted by first name, last name. As you type the letters, the list shrinks based on matches. Figure 4-9 illustrates how this works.

2. **Scroll and highlight the name from the list of matches.**

   If you have multiple matches, slide the screen to scroll through the list to find the person's name.

Figure 4-9:
Enter more
letters to
shorten the
potential
contact list
search.

3. **Press the menu key.**

   A menu appears.

4. **Touch-press one of the possible actions shown in Figure 4-10:**

   • *Activity Log:* Opens a screen listing e-mails, calls, and SMS messages you've made to the contact.

   • *Email:* Starts a new e-mail message. See Chapter 7 for more information.

   • *PIN:* Starts a new PIN-to-PIN message, which is a messaging feature unique to BlackBerry. With it, you can send a quick message to someone who has a BlackBerry. See Chapter 8 for more details about PIN-to-PIN messaging.

   • *Call:* Uses Phone to dial the number.

   • *SMS:* Starts a new *Short Messaging Service (SMS)* message, which is used in cellphones. See Chapter 8 for more details about SMS.

   • *Send as Attachment:* Starts a new e-mail message attaching the contacts. See Chapter 7 for more information.

If you have a finger-fumble and press a key in error, press the escape key once to return to the original list (the one showing all your contacts), or press the menu key and touch-press View All.

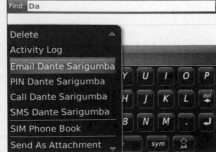

Figure 4-10:
You get
action
options for
the selected
contact.

You're not hallucinating: Sometimes Email *<contact name>* or Call *<contact name>* appears on the menu, and sometimes it doesn't. Contacts knows when to show those menu options. If a contact has a phone number, Call *<contact name>* and SMS *<contact name>* show up, and the same is true for e-mail and the *personal identification number (PIN)*. In fact, this list of actions is a convenient way to find out whether you have particular information — a phone number or an e-mail address — for a particular contact.

In a corporate environment, your BlackBerry Enterprise Server administrator might disable PIN-to-PIN messaging because it doesn't go to the corporate e-mail servers and, therefore, can't be monitored. If this is the case, the menu option PIN*<contact name>* won't appear even though you entered PIN information for your contacts. Note that you can still receive a PIN-to-PIN message, but you can't send one.

Organizing Your Contacts

You've been diligent by adding your contacts to your Contacts, and your list has been growing at a pretty good clip. It now has all the contact information for your business colleagues, clients, and (of course) family and friends. In fact, your Contacts has grown so much that it holds hundreds of contacts, and it's taking more time to find somebody.

Imagine that you've just seen an old acquaintance and you want to greet the person by name. You know that if you see the name you'd recognize it. The trouble is that your list has 300-plus names, which would take so long to scroll through — so long, in fact, that this acquaintance would surely come up to you in the meantime, forcing you to hide the fact that you can't remember his name. (How embarrassing.) In this scenario, the tried-and-true Find feature wouldn't be much help. What you need is a smaller pool of names to search through.

This isn't rocket science. You'll want to do one of the following:

✔ **Organize your contacts into groups:** Using groups (as every kindergarten teacher could tell you) is a way to arrange something (in your case, contacts) to make them more manageable. How you arrange your groups is up to you. You should base the principle on whatever makes sense to you and fits the group you set up. For example, you can place all your customer contacts within a Clients group and family members in a Family group.

✔ **Set up your contacts so you can filter them:** Use the Filter feature in combination with BlackBerry's Categories. (Categories is labeling your contacts to make it easy to filter them.) The Filter feature narrows the Contacts list to such an extent that you have to only scroll down and find your contact — no need to type search keywords, in other words.

Whether you use the Group or Filter feature is up to you. You find out how to use both methods in the next sections of this chapter.

Creating a group

A BlackBerry *group* in Contacts — as opposed to any other kind of group you can imagine — is just a simple category. In other words, a group arranges your contacts into subsets without affecting the contact entries themselves. In Contacts itself, a group shows up in the contact list just like any other contact. The only wrinkle here is that when you select the group, the contacts associated with that group — and only the contacts associated with that group — appear onscreen.

Need some help visualizing how this works? Go ahead and create a group, following these steps:

1. **On the Home screen, touch-press the Contacts icon.**

   Contacts opens.

2. **Press the menu key.**

3. **Touch-press New Group.**

   A screen similar to that in Figure 4-11 appears. The top portion of the screen is where you type the group name, and the bottom portion is where you add members.

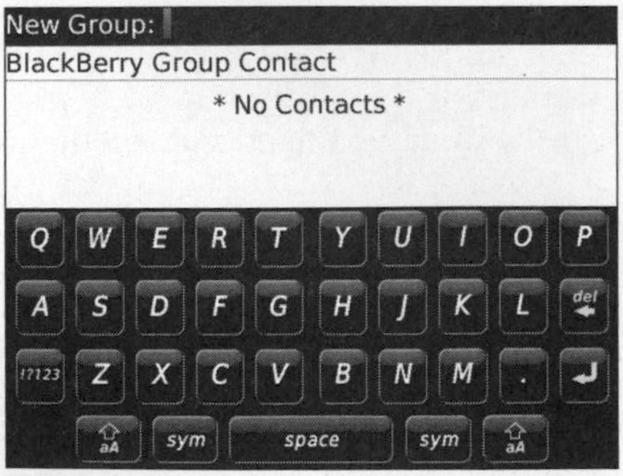

Figure 4-11:
An empty
screen
ready for
creating a
group.

4. **Type the name of the group in the New Group field.**

   You can name it anything.

5. **Press the menu key.**

6. **Touch-press Add Member.**

   The main Contacts list shows up in all its glory, ready to be pilfered.

7. **Touch-press the contact you want to add to your new Group list.**

You can't add a contact to a group if that contact doesn't have at least an e-mail address or a phone number. (It's very strict on this point.) Skirt this roadblock by editing that contact's information and putting in a fake (and clearly inactive) e-mail address, such as `notareal@ emailaddress.no`.

8. **Press the menu key.**

9. **Touch-press Continue.**

The name you just entered appears in your group list, as shown in Figure 4-12.

Figure 4-12: Your new group has one member.

10. **Repeat Steps 5–7 to add more friends to your list.**

11. **Press the menu key.**

12. **Touch-press Save Group.**

Your group is duly saved, and you can now see it listed on your main Contacts list.

Groups is a valuable tool to create an e-mail distribution list. Just make sure that you selected an e-mail address field on your members. Use a naming convention to easily distinguish it. Appending a *-DL* or *-Distribution List* on the name can quickly indicate it is a distribution list.

Using the Filter feature on your contacts

Are you a left brainer or a right brainer? Yankees fan or Red Sox fan? Innie or Outie? Dividing the world into categories is something everybody does (no divisions there), so it should come as no surprise that BlackBerry divides your contacts into distinct categories as well.

By default, two categories are set for you on the BlackBerry:

✔ Business

✔ Personal

Why stop at two? BlackBerry makes it easy to create more categories. In this section, you first find out how to categorize a contact, and then you see how to filter your Contacts list. Finally, you find out how to create categories.

Categorizing your contacts

Whether you're creating one or editing one, you can categorize a particular contact as long as you're in Edit mode.

If the trick is getting into Edit mode, it's a pretty simple trick. Here's how that's done:

1. **On the Home screen, touch-press the Contacts icon.**

   Contacts opens.

2. **Highlight the contact.**

3. **Press the menu key.**

4. **Touch-press Edit.**

   Contacts is in Edit mode for this particular contact, which is exactly where you want to be.

5. **Press the menu key.**

6. **Touch-press Categories.**

   A Categories list appears, as shown in Figure 4-13. By default, the list contains only the Business and the Personal categories.

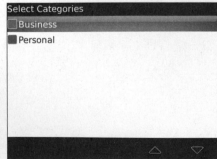

Figure 4-13:
Default
categories.

7. **Touch-press the Personal check box.**

8. **Press the menu key.**

9. **Touch-press Save.**

   You're back at the Edit screen for this particular contact.

10. **Press the menu key.**

11. **Touch-press Save.**

You now have one — count 'em, one — contact with Personal as its category, which means you can filter your Contacts list by using a category. Here's how:

1. **On the Home screen, touch-press the Contacts icon.**

2. **Press the menu key.**

3. **Touch-press Filter.**

   Your Categories list appears. If you haven't added any categories in the meantime, you see only the default Business and Personal categories.

4. **Touch-press the Personal check box.**

   A mark appears in the check box, and your Contacts list shrinks to the contacts in the Personal category, as shown in Figure 4-14.

Figure 4-14:
The
Contacts
list after
you apply a
filter.

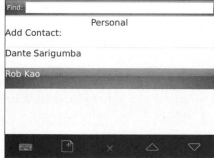

As you add contacts to a category, you can use Find. Enter the first few letters of the name to further narrow the contact search. If you need a refresher on how Find works, see the "Looking for Someone?" section earlier in this chapter.

Adding a category

Whoever thought the default categories — Business and Personal — were enough for the complexities of the real world probably didn't know many people. BlackBerry makes it easy to add categories, so you can divide your world as much as you like:

1. **On the Home screen, touch-press Contacts.**

2. **Press the menu key.**

3. **Touch-press Filter.**

    You get a view of the default categories. Refer to Figure 4-13.

4. **Press the menu key.**

5. **Touch-press New.**

    A pop-up screen asks you to name the category.

6. **Type a name for your category in the Name field.**

7. **Touch-press Enter.**

    The category is automatically saved. The Filter screen lists all the categories, including the one you just created. Just press the escape key to get back to the Contacts main screen.

Setting preferences

Vanilla, anyone? Some days you'll wish that your Contacts list was sorted differently. For example, there's the day when you need to find the guy who works for ABC Company but has a foreign name that you can hardly pronounce, let alone spell. What's a body to do?

You're in luck. Contacts Options navigates some out-of-the-ordinary situations. Figure 4-15 shows the Contacts Options screen. Despite its simplicity, it provides you with three important options that change Contacts behavior:

✔ **Sort By:** Changes the way the list is sorted. You can use First Name, Last Name, or Company. Touch-press the field to view and select from the possible choices. Remember that guy from ABC Company? You can use the Sort By option to sort by Company. By doing that, all contacts from ABC Company are listed next to each other and with any luck the guy's name will jump out at you.

✔ **Separators:** Allows you to change the dividers on the Contacts list. It's purely aesthetics but check it out, you might like the stripes.

✔ **Allow Duplicate Names:** Self-explanatory. If you turn this on, you can have multiple people who happen to share the same name in your Contacts. If you disable this option, you get a warning when you try to add a name that matches one already on your list. Maybe you're just tired and mistakenly try to add the same person twice to your list? Then again, sometimes people just have the same name. We recommend keeping the default value of Yes, allowing you to have contacts with the same names.

✔ **Confirm Delete:** Displays a confirmation screen for all contact deletions.

Always keep this feature turned on for normal usage. Because there are many ways you could delete somebody from your Contacts, this feature is a good way of minimizing accidents.

How do you change any of these options? The fields behave like any other on a BlackBerry application. Simply touch-press the field, and a menu allows you to select the possible option values. For example, Figure 4-16 shows the possible Sort By fields.

Contacts Options

Views

Sort By: First Name ▾

Separators: Lines ▾

Actions

Allow Duplicate Names: Yes ▾

Confirm Delete: Yes ▾

△   ▽

Figure 4-15:
Choose your
sort type
here.

Contacts Options

Views

Sort By: First Name ▾
         Last Name
Separators: Company

Actions

Allow Duplicate Names: Yes ▾

Confirm Delete: Yes ▾

△   ▽

Figure 4-16:
The Sort
By field
options.

Sharing a Contact

Suppose you want to share your contact information with a friend who also has a BlackBerry. A *vCard* — virtual (business) card — is your answer and can make your life a lot easier. In BlackBerry Land, a vCard is a contact in your Contacts that you send to someone as an attachment to an e-mail.

At the receiving end, the BlackBerry (being the smart device that it is) recognizes the attachment and informs the BlackBerry owner that she has the option of saving it, making it available for her viewing pleasure in Contacts.

Sending a vCard

Because a vCard is nothing more than a Contacts contact attached to an e-mail, sending a vCard is a piece of cake. (Of course, you do need to make sure that your recipient has a BlackBerry device to receive the information.)

Here's how you go about sending a vCard:

1. **On the Home screen, touch-press the Messages icon.**

   Messages opens.

2. **Press the menu key.**

3. **Touch-press Compose Email.**

   The new message screen appears, allowing you to compose a new e-mail.

4. **In the To field, start typing the name of the person you want to receive this vCard.**

5. **When you see the name in the drop-down list, touch-press it.**

   You see an e-mail screen with the name you just selected as the To recipient.

6. **Type the subject and message.**

7. **Press the menu key.**

8. **Touch-press Attach Contact.**

   Contacts opens.

9. **Touch-press the name of the person whose contact information you want attached.**

   The e-mail composition screen reappears, and an icon that looks like a book indicates that the e-mail now contains your attachment. Now all you have to do is send your e-mail.

10. **Press the menu key.**

11. **Touch-press Send.**

    You just shared the specified contact information. (Don't you feel right neighborly now?)

Receiving a vCard

If you get an e-mail that has a contact attachment, here's how to save it to your Contacts:

1. **On the Home screen, touch-press the Messages icon.**

2. **Touch-press the e-mail that contains the vCard.**

   The e-mail with the vCard attachment opens.

3. **Touch-press the attachment.**

4. **Press the menu key.**

5. **Touch-press View Attachment.**

   The vCard appears.

6. **Press the menu key.**

7. **Touch-press Add to Contacts.**

   The vCard is saved and is available in your BlackBerry Storm Contacts.

Searching for Somebody Outside Your Contacts

Does your employer provide your BlackBerry Storm? Do you use Outlook or Lotus Notes on your desktop machine at work? If you answer yes to both of these questions, this section is for you.

BlackBerry Contacts allows you to search for people in your organization, basically through this software:

- ✔ Microsoft Exchange (for Outlook)
- ✔ IBM Domino (for Notes)
- ✔ Novell GroupWise

Exchange, Domino, and GroupWise serve the same purposes: namely, to facilitate e-mail delivery in a corporate environment and to enable access to a database of names.

For you techies out there, these databases are called Global Address Lists (GAL) in Exchange; Notes Address Books in Domino; and GroupWise Address Books in GroupWise.

If you want to search for somebody in your organization through a database of names, simply follow these steps:

1. **On the Home screen, touch-press the Contacts icon.**

2. **Press the menu key.**

3. **Touch-press Lookup.**

Some corporations might not enable the Lookup feature. Please check with your IT department for more information.

4. **Type the name you're searching for.**

5. **Press the enter key.**

You could enter the beginning characters of either a person's last or first name. You aren't searching your Contacts but your company's database, so this step might take some time.

For big organizations, we recommend being more precise when searching. For example, searching for *Dan* yields more hits than searching for *Daniel.* The more precise your search criteria, the fewer hits you'll get and the faster the search will be.

While the search is in progress, you see the word Lookup and the criteria you put in. For example, if you enter *Daniel,* the top row reads Lookup: Daniel. After the search is finished, BlackBerry displays the number of hits or matches: for example, 20 matches: Daniel.

6. **Touch-press the matches count.**

The matches appear. A header at the top of this screen details the matches displayed in the current screen as well as the total hits. For example, if the header reads something like Lookup Daniel (20 of 130 matches), 130 people in your organization have the name *Daniel,* and BlackBerry is displaying the first 20. You have the option of fetching more by pressing the menu key and touching Get More Results from the menu that appears.

You can add the listed name(s) to your Contacts by using the Add command (for the currently highlighted name) or the Add All command for all the names on the list. (As always, press the menu key.)

7. **Touch-press the person whose information you want to review.**

The person's contact information is displayed on a *read-only* screen, which means you can read it but not change it. You might see the person's title, e-mail address, work, mobile, and fax numbers, and the street address at work. Any of that information gives you confirmation about the person you're looking for. Of course, what shows up depends on the availability of this information in your company's database.

Chapter 5

Keeping Your Appointments

In This Chapter

▶ Seeing your schedule from different time frames

▶ Making your Calendar your own

▶ Scheduling a meeting

▶ Making and breaking appointments

To some folks, the key to being organized and productive is mastering time management (and we're not just talking about reading this book while you're commuting to work). Many know that the best way to organize their time is to use a calendar — a daily planner tool. Those who prefer digital to paper use a planner program on their PC — either installed on their hard drive or accessed through an Internet portal (such as Yahoo!). The smartest of the bunch, of course, use their BlackBerry Storm because it has the whole planner thing covered with its Calendar.

In this chapter, we show you how to keep your life (both personal and work) in order by managing your appointments with your BlackBerry Calendar. What's great about managing your time on a BlackBerry Storm? Your Storm is always with you.

Just remember that you won't have excuses anymore for forgetting that important quarterly meeting or Bertha's birthday bash.

Accessing BlackBerry Calendar

 BlackBerry Calendar is one of the BlackBerry Storm's core applications, like Contacts or Phone (read more about the others in Chapter 1), so it's easy to get to. From the Home screen, press the menu key and touch-press the Calendar icon on screen. *Voilà!* You have Calendar.

Choosing your Calendar view

The first time you open Calendar the Day view appears by default, as shown in Figure 5-1. However, you can change the Calendar view to one that works better for your needs:

Figure 5-1:
Day view in
Calendar.

- ✔ **Day:** A summary of your appointments for the day. By default, it lists all your appointments from 9 a.m. to 5 p.m.
- ✔ **Week:** This view shows you a seven-day summary view of your appointments. By using this view, you can see how busy you are in a particular week.
- ✔ **Month:** The Month view shows you every day of the month. You can't tell how many appointments are in a day, but you can see on which days you have appointments.

✔ **Agenda:** The Agenda view is a bit different from the other views. It isn't a time-based view like the others; it basically lists your upcoming appointments. And in the list, you can see details of the appointments, such as where and when.

Different views (like the ones shown in Figure 5-2) offer a different focus on your schedule. Select the view you want based on your scheduling needs and preferences. If your life is a little more complicated, you can even use a combination of views for a full grasp of your schedule.

Figure 5-2: Change your Calendar view to fit your life.

10 Oct 2008			Week 41		10:25	
October						
M	T	W	T	F	S	S
29	30	1	2	3	4	5
6	7	8	9	10	11	12
13	14	15	16	17	18	19
20	**21**	**22**	**23**	**24**	25	26
27	28	29	30	31	1	2
3	4	5	6	7	8	9

To switch between different Calendar views, simply follow these steps:

1. **From the Home screen, touch-press the Calendar icon.**

   The Calendar application is called up in its default view — Day view (more than likely).

2. **Press the menu key and then touch-press on the view of your choice from the menu that appears.**

   If you start from Month view, your choices are View Day, View Week, and View Agenda (see Figure 5-3).

Figure 5-3:
The
Calendar
menu lets
you select
different
views.

Moving between time frames

Depending on what Calendar view you're in, you can easily move to the previous or next day, week, month, or year. For example, if you're looking at June in the Month view, you can move to May or July. In fact, if you like to look at things long term, you can jump ahead (or back) a year at a time. See Figure 5-4.

Figure 5-4:
Move
between
months or
years in
Month view.

Without using the menu, you can quickly move to the next "page." The bottom-right hand corner of the screen has back and forward arrows; try them in each time frame view (Day view, Week view, Month view).

You have similar flexibility when it comes to the other Calendar views. See Table 5-1 for a summary of what's available.

Table 5-1	Moving between Views
Calendar View	*Move Between*
Day	Days and weeks
Week	Weeks
Month	Months and years
Agenda	Days

You can always go to today's date regardless of what Calendar view you're in. Just press the menu key and touch-press Today. Onscreen, the icon that looks like number one gets you back to Today. Also, you can jump to any date by pressing the menu key and touch-pressing Go to Date. To change the date, type the desired day, month, and year, as shown in Figure 5-5.

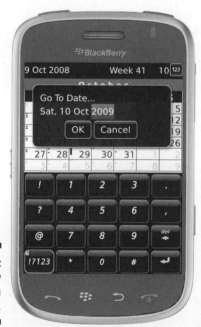

Figure 5-5: Go to any date you want.

Customizing your Calendar

To change the default view in your Calendar — from Day to Month, for example — Calendar Options is the answer.

To get to Calendar Options, follow these steps:

1. **Open Calendar.**

2. **Press the menu key and touch-press Options⇨General Options.**

   You see choices similar to the ones shown in Table 5-2.

Table 5-2	Calendar Options
Option	*Description*
Formatting	
First Day of Week	The day that first appears in your Week view.
Start of Day	The time of day that defines your start of day in Day view. The default is 9 a.m. If you change this to 8 a.m., for example, your Day view starts at 8 a.m. instead of 9 a.m.
End of Day	The time of the day that defines the end of day in Day view. The default is 5 p.m. If you change this to 6 p.m., for example, your Day view ends at 6 p.m. instead of 5 p.m.
Views	
Initial View	Specify the Calendar view that you see when opening Calendar.
Show Free Time in Agenda View	If Yes, this field allows an appointment-free date to appear in the Agenda view. If No, the Agenda view doesn't show days you don't have appointments.
Show End Time in Agenda View	If Yes, this field shows the end time of each appointment in the Agenda view. If No, the Agenda view shows only the start time of each appointment.
Actions	
Snooze	The delay before a reminder appears. The default is 5 minutes.
Default Reminder	How long before your appointment you're notified. The default is 15 minutes.

Option	Description
Actions	
Enable Quick Entry	Day view only. Make a new appointment by typing characters.
Confirm Delete	Determines whether you're prompted for confirmation upon appointment deletion.
Keep Appointments	The number of days your StormCalendar item is saved. We recommend Never.
Show Tasks	A scheduled task appears on your Calendar just like a Calendar event. *Note:* A scheduled task is a task with a due date. See Chapter 6.
Show Alarms	You can see alarms in your Calendar if you set this option to Yes.

Managing multiple Calendars

Like your e-mail accounts, you might have multiple Calendars. For example, you might have a Calendar from your day job and you might have a Calendar from your personal life or softball club that you belong to. Whatever the reason, your BlackBerry Storm has a great way for you to manage this.

You can assign different color squares to represent different Calendars; this gives you a better view of which event belongs to which Calendar. For example, you can have your day job Calendar as red and your softball club Calendar as green. When you have two events conflict at the same time slot, you can better prioritize with the color. See Figure 5-6.

Follow these steps to change the color of each Calendar:

1. **Open Calendar.**

2. **Press the menu key and touch-press Options.**

3. **Touch-press a Calendar of your choice.**

    The Calendar Properties screen opens.

4. **Touch-press the colored square and then touch-press the desired color.**

5. **Press the menu key.**

6. **Touch-press Save.**

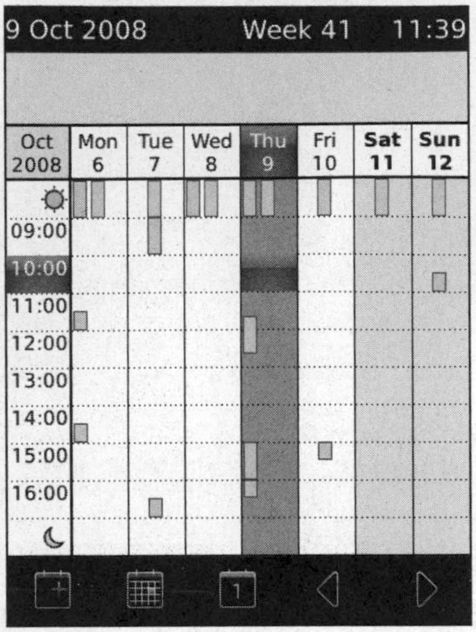

9 Oct 2008				Week 41			11:39

Figure 5-6: Day view in Calendar, showing different colors for different Calendars.

All Things Appointment: Adding, Opening, and Deleting

After you master the different Calendar views (and that should take you all of about two minutes), and you have Calendar customized to your heart's content (another three minutes, tops), it's time (pun intended) to set up, review, and delete appointments. We also show you how to set up a meeting with clients or colleagues.

Creating an appointment

Setting up a new appointment is easy. You need only one piece of information: when your appointment occurs. Of course, you can easily add related information about the appointment:

- Meeting's purpose
- Location
- Additional notes

TIP

In addition to your standard, one-time, limited-duration meeting, you can set all-day appointments. The BlackBerry can assist you in setting *recurring* (repeating) meetings as well as reminders. Sweet!

Creating a one-time appointment

To add a new one-time appointment, follow these steps:

1. **Open Calendar.**

2. **Press the menu key and touch-press New.**

   The New Appointment screen appears, as shown in Figure 5-7.

   You can also touch-press the bottom left icon with a plus sign to open the New Appointment screen.

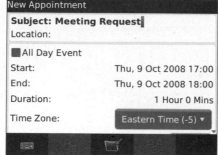

Figure 5-7:
Set an appointment here.

3. **Fill in the appointment information.**

   Type the information regarding your appointment in the appropriate spaces. You should at least enter the time and the subject of your appointment.

4. **Press the menu key and touch-press Save.**

   Your appointment is now available from any Calendar view.

You can have more than one appointment in the same time slot. BlackBerry lets you decide which appointment you should go for and which one you conveniently forget.

Creating an all-day appointment

If your appointment is an all-day event — you're in corporate training or have an all-day doctor's appointment — mark the All Day Event check box in the New Appointment screen.

Setting your appointment reminder time

You can associate any Calendar appointment with a reminder alert — either a vibration or a beep, depending on how you set things up in your profile. (For more on profiles, see Chapter 3.) You can have *no* reminder for an appointment.

Create a reminder this way: From the New Appointment screen, simply scroll to the Reminder field and select a reminder time anywhere from none to 1 week before your appointment time.

Profile is simply another useful feature that allows you to customize how your BlackBerry alerts you when an *event* occurs. Examples of events are an e-mail, a phone call, or an appointment reminder.

By default, whatever reminder alert you set goes off 15 minutes before the event. But you don't have to stick with the default. You can choose your own default reminder time:

1. **Open Calendar.**

2. **Press the menu key and touch-press Options.**

   The Calendar Options screen comes up.

3. **Touch-press Default Reminder.**

4. **Touch-press a default reminder time anywhere from none to 1 week before your appointment.**

   From now on, any new appointment has the reminder you set up. Assuming a reminder time other than none (you're on your own, then!), a dialog box like the one in Figure 5-8 appears, letting you know an appointment is coming up.

Figure 5-8:
You get a reminder dialog box if you want.

Creating a recurring appointment

Everyone has some repeating appointments: birthdays, anniversaries, taking out the trash every Thursday at 7:30 a.m. You can set up recurring appointments based on daily, weekly, monthly, or yearly recurrences.

You can define an Every field for all types; see Figure 5-9. For example, say you have an appointment that recurs every nine days:

Set the Recurrence field to Daily.

Set the Every field to 9.

Figure 5-9:
An appointment recurring every nine days.

Depending on what you select in the Recurrence field, you have the option to fill in other fields:

- **Weekly:** You can fill in the Day of the Week field.

- **Monthly or Yearly:** The Relative Date check box is available. With this checked, you can ensure that your appointment recurs relative to today's date. For example, if you choose the following, your appointment occurs every two months on the third Sunday until July 31, 2012:

  Start: Sunday, June 17, 2010 at 12 p.m.

  End: Sunday, June 17, 2010 at 1 p.m.

  Recurrence: Monthly

  Every: 2

  Relative Date: Selected

  End: Saturday, July 31, 2012

On the other hand, if all options in our example remain the same except you don't select Relative Date, your appointment occurs every two months, on the 18th of the month, until July 31, 2012.

If all this "relative" talk has you dizzy, don't worry: The majority of your appointments won't be as complicated as this.

Opening an appointment

After you set an appointment, you can view it in a couple of ways:

- ✔ Click the Open box in the Reminder dialog box. Refer to Figure 5-8.
- ✔ From Calendar, touch-press the exact time of your appointment.

While looking at an appointment, you can designate a new appointment time or a new appointment location and then save.

Deleting an appointment

That meeting you were dreading got cancelled. Whoopee! Deleting an appointment is straightforward. When in Day or Week view, simply finger scroll to the appointment that you want to delete, press the menu key, and touch-press Delete from the menu that appears.

Or you can touch-press the appointment to bring it up, and then touch-press the bottom-right icon that has a red x to delete the appointment.

If the appointment you're deleting is recurring, a dialog box asks whether you want to delete

- ✔ All occurrences of this appointment
- ✔ Just this particular occurrence, as shown in Figure 5-10

Figure 5-10:
You can delete all occurrences or just the single instance of a recurring appointment.

Appointments versus Meetings

Technically, any event is as an appointment, whether it's your friend's birthday or a doctor's appointment. However, when you invite people or are invited to a meeting (whether it's face-to-face or via phone), that appointment becomes a *meeting*.

Sending a meeting request

Sending a meeting request to others is similar to creating a Calendar appointment:

1. **Open Calendar.**
2. **Press the menu key and then touch-press New.**
3. **Fill in the key appointment information.**
4. **Press the menu key and then touch-press Invite Attendee.**

    You're taken to Address Book to select your meeting attendee.

5. **From Address Book:**

    • *If you have contacts in your Address Book:* Touch-press the contact you want to invite.

    • *If you don't yet have contacts or the one you want isn't in your Address Book:* Choose the Use Once option to type the appropriate e-mail address to Calendar.

    You see the attendees in your Calendar meeting notice.

6. **Press the menu key and then touch-press Save.**

    Your meeting attendees receive an e-mail, inviting them to your meeting.

Responding to a meeting request

Whether for work or for a casual event, you've likely received a meeting request by e-mail. You were probably asked to choose one of three options: Accept, Tentative, or Decline. (If it's from your boss for an all-staff meeting and you just can't afford to decline again because it's so close to Christmas bonus time, that's an Accept.)

You can accept any meeting request from your managers or colleagues on your BlackBerry just as you would on your desktop PC. Upon reading the e-mail on your BlackBerry, choose one of the following in the Messages application:

✔ Accept
✔ Tentative
✔ Decline

Your response is sent in an e-mail. We go into more detail about the Messages application in Chapter 7.

If you choose Accept or Tentative, the meeting is added to your Calendar automatically. If you have a change of heart, you can delete the declined event and it disappears from your Calendar. You can do this by going back to the Calendar event and touch-press Decline from the menu.

Setting your meeting dial-in number

In this global economy, many of us have colleagues and friends that are located in another country or even on another continent. So, when it comes to having a meeting, usually it is through a phone conference that involves a dial-in number, moderator code (if you are the moderator), and participation code.

Your BlackBerry Storm makes storing and displaying these numbers easy when you're creating a new appointment in the BlackBerry Calendar.

To set your phone conference dial-in details, follow these steps:

1. **Open Calendar.**
2. **Press the menu key and touch-press Options.**
3. **Touch-press Conference Call Options.**

   A screen similar to Figure 5-11 appears.
4. **Enter the appropriate numbers.**
5. **Press the menu key and touch-press Save.**

Figure 5-11:
Setting up
Conference
Call dial-in
details.

The next time you create a new appointment with a conference call, the conference number shows up.

Chapter 6

Making Notes and Calculations

*Y*ou know what a memo pad is. Most people take them to meetings. Yes, you take them to those looong meetings. Bored and need to stay awake? Your memo pad is the answer. You can draw faces, doodle fanciful designs, or even write a poem, all the while pretending to listen to your colleagues. Why do people like to call for meetings? Let's get everybody in a room and talk about something that doesn't concern them. Just lovely, isn't it?

What we describe in this chapter is your e-memo pad for taking notes — the aptly named *MemoPad* — on your BlackBerry Storm.

Your BlackBerry Storm has another handy application that saves you from having to stuff yet another gizmo in your bag: its built-in Calculator, which we talk about in this chapter as well.

Taking a MemoPad

MemoPad on your BlackBerry Storm can prove handy, indeed. If nothing else, use it to jot down important notes and ideas you might forget. How much frustration must you endure for not remembering a fleeting thought? Like when you forget why you actually called somebody. Writing down your thoughts is the best way to remember. Use your handy-dandy BlackBerry Storm to record them.

In upcoming sections, we explore how to jot down notes by using MemoPad as well as how to effectively organize your notes and come back to them quickly by using filters. We also throw in tips on how to print your notes.

Accessing MemoPad

Accessing MemoPad is a snap. Depending on the theme you're using, you can get to it right from the Home screen or through the Applications folder. With the Verizon theme, you access MemoPad through the Applications icon as shown on the left in Figure 6-1. The MemoPad screen appears, as shown on the right in Figure 6-1.

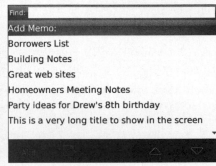

Figure 6-1: Open MemoPad here.

Jotting down notes

Recording notes is a breeze.

1. **Touch-press Add Memo located on the top of the screen, below Find.**

   An empty memo screen comes up, as shown in Figure 6-2. A line divides the screen.

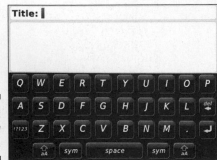

Figure 6-2: Start a new note here.

When entering notes, always hold your BlackBerry Storm lengthwise *(landscape)* to use the QWERTY virtual keypad, which is easier and quicker for typing.

2. Enter the title in the top field.

Your MemoPad list is sorted alphabetically, so choose a helpful first word when entering the title. Stay away from starting with *A, An, The, This,* and similar words. Briefly describe the subject. If you use long words, five words are ideal; otherwise, six words can fit.

Of course, you can enter more than six words — or as many as you want — but remember that the BlackBerry screen isn't wide. MemoPad displays the title as one line in the main MemoPad screen, which is the Find list. If your note title is longer than the width of the screen, the title is truncated with an ellipsis (. . .) at its end.

3. Type your memo in the bottom part.

Your memo can be another *War and Peace* as long as your BlackBerry can store it.

Just like jotting down new memos, you can access all your memos easily in the MemoPad list and act on them by using the options accessible in the bottom of the screen, as shown on the left of Figure 6-3, or through the menu, as shown in the right of Figure 6-3. You can edit the memo by touch-pressing A|cd, forward it by touch-pressing the memo icon with the right arrow, or delete the memo by touch-pressing the Delete (X) icon. Remember that just like in other applications, the menu is always available by pressing the menu key. The menu that appears is in context with the currently selected memo, which allows you to Forward As, Edit, and Delete (see the right side of Figure 6-3).

Just like in Contacts and Messages, the menu is always available by pressing the menu key.

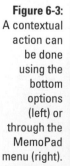

Figure 6-3: A contextual action can be done using the bottom options (left) or through the MemoPad menu (right).

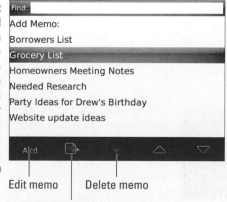

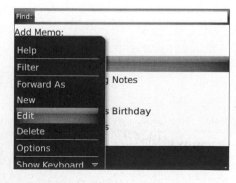

Edit memo   Delete memo

Forward memo

Viewing and editing your notes

Obviously, you jot a memo for future reference. Viewing or editing the memo is the next logical step. After MemoPad is open, touch-press the memo you want, and a screen displaying your memo shows up. You can edit your memo right on this screen.

If you're not happy with the font size, whether it's too small or too big, see Chapter 3 for details on how to customize display fonts. MemoPad is using the global preferences defined in Options under the Screen/Keyboard section.

Deleting your notes

Face it, half the sticky notes you leave on your desk are no longer relevant. Your MemoPad is no different. Delete what you don't need. Touch-press the scroll arrow keys at the bottom of the screen to highlight the memo you want to delete from your MemoPad list, and touch-press the Delete (X) icon in the bottom of the screen. Ready to say goodbye? Touch-press Delete from the confirmation screen. Your memo is gone.

The confirmation screen is a feature common to all out-of-the-box BlackBerry Storm applications such as Contacts, Tasks, and Calendar. It diminishes the accidental deletion of records. You can enable or disable this feature.

Disabling the confirmation screen is useful when you're getting rid of lots of memos and don't want to be bothered by it. (Be sure to turn the feature back on when you're finished deleting.)

To turn off this feature, just do the following:

1. **Go to the MemoPad Options screen, and touch-press the Confirm Delete field.**

   The screen shows your two choices: Yes and No. No means you want to toggle off the Confirmation screen.

2. **Touch-press No.**

   The MemoPad Options screen updates to show No in the Confirm Delete field.

3. **Press the menu key and then touch-press Save.**

   The MemoPad application applies the changes you made.

Another field you can see from the MemoPad Options screen is Number of Entries. This field is just informational, showing you how many memos you have in your MemoPad application.

Finding a note — quickly

The Find field is always on the main MemoPad screen. Just like Contacts (see Chapter 4), you can use this feature to find a note by typing in the field next to Find. (Ah, the importance of good note-naming becomes clearer all the time.)

In the Find field, start typing what you think your note is titled. The list below shrinks, based on matches. A *match* is based on the starting letters of the subjects. As you type more letters in the Find field, your MemoPad note list is filtered more. For example, if you type **bi**, you see notes with titles like *bid night* and *birthday,* as shown in Figure 6-4.

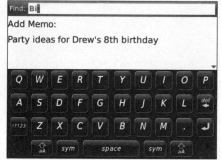

Figure 6-4:
Search
notes here.

Organizing your notes

MemoPad is easy and helpful; you can make it more effective by organizing your notes list. Like in Contacts and Tasks, you can group your notes and then show a list of contacts based on a grouping. Simply define a group — a *category* — and then assign that category to a note.

Creating a category

Categories are common to most BlackBerry Storm applications and categories go across applications. For example, a category you see in MemoPad is the same category you see in Tasks or Contacts. You can access a category from the menu of any of these BlackBerry applications. To create a category from MemoPad, follow these steps:

1. **From the Applications folder screen, touch-press MemoPad.**

   MemoPad opens and you see the list of your notes.

   You can find the Applications folder from the Home screen by pressing the menu key.

2. **Press the menu key and then touch-press Filter.**

   A screen lists all the available categories. By default, BlackBerry Storm gives you Personal and Business categories as shown in Figure 6-5.

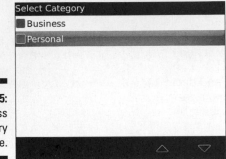

Figure 6-5:
Touch-press
a category
here.

3. **Press the menu key and then touch-press New.**

   A New Category screen appears.

4. **Enter the category name in the text field.**

5. **Touch-press the enter key.**

   The new category name appears in the list of category names.

6. **Press the menu key and touch-press Close.**

Assigning a category

You can assign categories to your notes when you create or edit a memo. Either way, the steps are the same.

Follow these steps to edit a memo and assign a category:

1. **In MemoPad, touch-press the memo you want to edit.**

2. **Press the menu key.**

3. **Touch-press Categories.**

   A list of categories appears.

4. **Touch-press the category you want.**

   The highlighted category is selected, which means your memo will be associated to this category. You can select as many categories as you want.

5. **Press the menu key.**

6. **Touch-press Save.**

   The Note screen returns. Although the assignment is now in your memo, it doesn't stay until you save the note itself.

7. **Press the menu key.**

8. **Touch-press Save.**

   Your note is saved and attached to the category you chose.

If you're working in MemoPad and decide to delete a category, you lose that category and all its assignments in the other applications, such as Contacts. (The Contacts contact is still intact, but without the category assignment.)

Filtering the list

Time to see just how easy MemoPad can make your life. Finding a note that belongs to a category (see the preceding section on assigning a note category) is just a touch-press away. To filter your notes list for a certain category, follow these steps:

1. **From the Applications folder, touch-press MemoPad.**

   MemoPad opens.

2. **Press the menu key.**

3. **Touch-press Filter.**

   A screen appears with the available categories.

4. **Touch-press the category you want.**

   Your filtered list appears. Note that the list now has the category name as the heading, as shown in Figure 6-6.

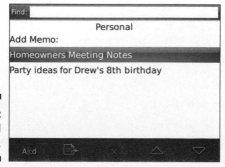

Figure 6-6:
Filtered
notes.

Printing notes

Okay, you got us. Out of the box, you can't exactly print notes directly from BlackBerry Storm. However, if you search for a BlackBerry printer online, you see lots of options.

Following are some solutions:

- ✔ **Third-party applications (Bluetooth):** You install a commercial application, such as Content Beamer from `www.thinprint.com`, to your BlackBerry Storm. Such applications use a Bluetooth connection to a printer that also works with Bluetooth.

- ✔ **Third-party applications (Internet/e-mail based):** A server-based application that connects to your e-mail server prints any e-mail attachment. In your BlackBerry, you have to install an application allowing you to send the command to print. A sample of such an application is MasterDoc for BlackBerry at `www.dynoplex.com/printing_master.shtml`.

- ✔ **Through your desktop PIM software:** Even if you buy an application that allows you to print from your BlackBerry, you still need a computer to process that command. Having the Bluetooth option for printing is convenient. If you're cost conscious, however, the best way is to sync your device with an application, such as Outlook or Outlook Express, which features an equivalent MemoPad-type application that you can sync with BlackBerry MemoPad. From there, you can then print your notes. In Chapter 14, we describe in detail how to connect your BlackBerry to a desktop computer and sync information between your BlackBerry and your desktop application.

Calculating

Sure, calculators are everywhere and readily accessible. But using the BlackBerry Storm Calculator is so easy!

Of course, Calculator performs just like you expect it to, but stick with us to see how easily you can use it to convert between metric and English measurement systems.

Accessing Calculator

Calculator is filed in the Applications folder (see Figure 6-7). You can easily pick it out because it looks like an old-fashioned calculator.

Just like other BlackBerry Storm applications, opening Calculator is a simple matter of touch-pressing its icon.

Using Calculator

Calculator has the standard number pad look that you're used to, as shown in Figure 6-8. Of course, you can do basic math. With the ability to touch-press the virtual keys, it should be as easy as using the traditional calculator. We recommend you hold the BlackBerry Storm lengthwise (landscape) to show all the keys. But if you have to hold it with a single hand (portrait), some keys have two functions. The upper portion is active by pressing Shift key and can be found on the bottom-left corner of the screen.

Figure 6-8:
Calculator
screen in
landscape
(left) and
portrait
(right) mode.

You'll undoubtedly note some nonnumeric keys in Calculator:

- ✔ **C:** Clear

- ✔ **CE:** Clear Entry

- ✔ **M-:** Memory Clear; clears the contents of the register

- ✔ **MR:** Memory Recall; reaches to the register and uses the number stored there

- ✔ **MS:** Memory Save; saves to the register

- ✔ **M+:** Memory Plus; adds a number to the register

- ✔ **1/x:** Invert multiplication (one divided by the entered number)

Converting between English and metric systems

When you're faced with an unfamiliar measurement system — say, liters versus gallons or miles versus kilometers — you'll probably need help converting. Conveniently enough, your BlackBerry Calculator can help you. From its menu, you can quickly convert measurements from English to metric or vice versa.

Display the conversion menu (shown in Figure 6-9) by pressing the menu key.

As an example, to convert 20 kilometers to miles, follow these steps:

1. **From the Applications folder, touch-press Calculator.**

   Calculator opens.

2. **Touch-press the digits of the numeral you want to convert.**

   Your first numeral (20 in this example) appears in the numeral field of the Calculator screen.

3. **Press the menu key.**

4. **Touch-press the From Metric menu item (see Figure 6-9).**

   The menu screen with the conversion choices appears, as shown in Figure 6-10. Table 6-1 displays these conversion units.

   The arrow directions tell you the direction of the conversion. If you touch-press To Metric compared with From Metric (as in this example), the arrow direction is reversed.

5. **Touch-press km → mi from the menu.**

   The screen displays the results of the conversion — 12.427424, in this case.

Figure 6-9:
Select the conversion method between measurement systems.

Figure 6-10:
You can convert these units in Calculator.

Table 6-1		Conversion Units
Metric	*English*	*Convert Between*
In	Cm	Inches and centimeters
Ft	M	Feet and meters
Yd	M	Yards and meters
Mi	Km	Miles and kilometers
Lb	Kg	Pounds and kilograms
F	C	Fahrenheit and Celsius
US gal	L	US gallons and liters
UK gal	L	UK gallons and liters

Part III
Getting Multimedia and Online with Your Storm

The 5th Wave   By Rich Tennant

It's an e-mail from my mother. She wants me to know how happy she is for us.

In this part . . .

Here's the good stuff — using your BlackBerry for e-mail (Chapter 7), for text messaging (Chapter 8), going online and Web surfing (Chapter 9), and making those all-important phone calls (Chapter 10). Explore the camera (Chapter 11) that comes with the BlackBerry Storm and have fun with Storm's multimedia capabilities (Chapter 12). Get directions from the BlackBerry GPS (Chapter 13).

Chapter 7

You've Got (Lots of) E-Mail

Your BlackBerry Storm brings a fresh new face to the convenience and ease of use that are associated with e-mail. You can direct mail to your BlackBerry from up to ten e-mail accounts, including the likes of Yahoo! and AOL. You can set up an e-mail signature, configure e-mail filters, and search for e-mail messages.

In this chapter we show you how to use and manage your BlackBerry's mail capabilities to its full potential. From setup to sorts, we have you covered here.

Getting Up and Running with E-Mail

Regardless of your network service provider (such as T-Mobile, or Rogers, or Vodafone), you can set up your BlackBerry to receive mail from at least one of your current e-mail accounts. Thus, with whatever address you use to send and receive e-mail from your PC (Yahoo!, Gmail, and so on), you can hook up your BlackBerry to use that same e-mail address. Instead of checking your Gmail at the Google site, for example, you can get it on your BlackBerry. Is your company running a BES and MS Exchange server, but didn't think to give you a company BlackBerry? No worries, you can still get your e-mail via the BlackBerry Desktop Redirector. Keep reading.

Most network service providers allow you to connect up to ten e-mail accounts to your BlackBerry. This capability provides you with the convenience of one central point from which you get all your e-mail. Such convenience!

Using the BlackBerry Internet Service client

You can pull together all your e-mail accounts into one by using the *BlackBerry Internet Service client* (formerly known as the BlackBerry Web client). The BlackBerry Internet Service client allows you to

- ✔ **Manage up to ten e-mail accounts:** See the next section, "Combining your e-mail accounts into one."

- ✔ **Use wireless e-mail reconciliation:** No more trying to match your BlackBerry e-mail against e-mail in your combined account(s). Just turn on wireless e-mail reconciliation and you're good to go. For more on this, see the upcoming section, "Enabling wireless reconciliation."

- ✔ **Create e-mail filters:** You can filter e-mails to get only those messages that you truly care about on your BlackBerry. See the "Filtering your e-mail" section, near the end of this chapter.

Think of the BlackBerry Internet Service client (also known simply as *Service client*) as an online e-mail account manager that doesn't keep your messages. Instead, it routes the e-mails from your other accounts to your BlackBerry (because it's directly connected to your BlackBerry).

Combining your e-mail accounts into one

To start herding e-mail accounts onto your BlackBerry, you must first run a setup program from the BlackBerry Internet Service client.

You can access the Service client from your BlackBerry or from your desktop computer. To do so, you need the URL that is specific to your network service. Contact your network service provider (T-Mobile, Verizon, and so on) directly to get that information.

After you've logged into the Service client, you should see a screen similar to Figure 7-1. If your network provider has activated your BlackBerry, you should see one e-mail address: your BlackBerry's default address.

The Service client has three options on the left navigation bar:

- ✔ **E-mail Accounts:** Here you can add, edit, and delete e-mail accounts. In addition, you can set up filters and a signature for each address.

- ✔ **Change Handheld:** This option isn't used frequently. We don't cover it here.

- ✔ **Service Books:** This option isn't used frequently. We don't cover it here.

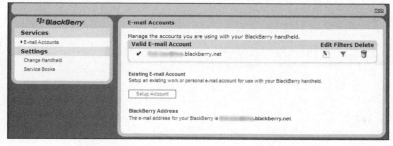

Figure 7-1:
Set up
an e-mail
account
here.

As mentioned, your BlackBerry already has a default e-mail address with which you can receive and send e-mail. If you don't have any other e-mail account that you want to meld into your BlackBerry e-mail account, simply skip to the upcoming "Customizing Your E-Mail" section.

Adding an e-mail account

We suggest that you first register and create your account by using your PC. Then for subsequent visits to the BlackBerry Internet Service client, you can use your BlackBerry. This way, you can minimize any errors or out-of-network coverage issues while setting up your account.

You can have up to ten e-mail accounts on your BlackBerry. To add an e-mail account to your BlackBerry account, follow these steps:

1. **From the BlackBerry Internet Service client (refer to Figure 7-1), click Setup Account.**

   You see the Add E-mail Account screen.

2. **Enter the address and login credentials for that e-mail address.**

   - The e-mail address is the address from which you want to receive e-mail, for example, `myid@yahoo.com`.

- The account login is the one you use to log into this particular e-mail account.

- The password is the one you use with the login.

3. Click the Next button.

You're finished. It's that easy!

You can also manage your accounts from your BlackBerry. From the Home screen, press the menu key and select Set Up Internet E-mail. The rest is pretty much the same on the BlackBerry as it is on a PC.

Using Desktop Redirector: How enterprising!

If you're a sole proprietor or consultant who works in a corporation that runs Exchange or Lotus and want to get enterprise (corporate) e-mails on your own BlackBerry, this section is for you.

Normally, to get enterprise e-mail your BlackBerry has to be configured with the *BlackBerry Enterprise Server (BES).* This is typical if your employer hands you a BlackBerry. However, if you work for a large company as a contractor, you probably won't get a BlackBerry from the company you work for.

When you want to get enterprise e-mail to avoid falling behind (especially if you don't work five days a week), you need Desktop Redirector. In order for you to do this, you first need to install BlackBerry Desktop Manager, which you can find out how to do in Chapter 14.

After you've installed Desktop Manager with Redirector, make sure that Redirector starts every time you boot up your PC.

Some corporations allow Desktop Redirector but some don't. Contact your IT department for proper setup.

Just a few caveats when using the Desktop Redirector:

- ✔ You get enterprise e-mail as long as your PC is turned on and have a connection to the Internet.

- ✔ When someone sends you an attachment, you can't retrieve it from your BlackBerry.

- ✔ When someone sends you a meeting notice, you can't accept or reject the invitation.

Customizing Your E-Mail

In this section we go over the details of the following e-mail configurations:

- ✔ Create an e-mail signature if you're tired of writing *Regards, John Smith* over and over to close an e-mail.

- ✔ After enabling e-mail reconciliation, whatever you see on your BlackBerry is what you get in your e-mail account(s). You no longer have to double-delete a message in both your BlackBerry and your e-mail account(s).

- ✔ Whether you're out of the office or want a quick response message sent to your senders, auto-replies is where you can specify the message. This feature is for enterprise users only.

Configuring your e-mail signature

By default, your e-mail signature is something like "Sent via My BlackBerry," which can be cool in the first week, showing off to people that you're a la mode with your BlackBerry. But sooner or later, you might not want people to know that you are out and about while answering e-mail. Or you might want something more personal.

Follow these steps to configure your e-mail signature by using the Service client:

1. **Log into Service client on your PC.**

   The BlackBerry Internet Service client appears. (Refer to Figure 7-1.)

2. **Click the Edit icon for the desired e-mail account.**

   The edit screen appears, as shown in Figure 7-2.

3. **In the Signature field, type the text for your e-mail signature.**

4. **Click Save.**

Because the internet connection might be spotty from your BlackBerry at times, we recommend that you first set up your signature on your PC.

Figure 7-2:
The e-mail
account edit
screen.

Enabling wireless reconciliation

With wireless reconciliation, you don't need to delete the same e-mail in two places. The two e-mail inboxes reconcile with each other, hence the term *wireless reconciliation*. Convenient, huh?

Enabling wireless e-mail synchronization

You can start wireless e-mail synchronization by configuring your BlackBerry:

1. **From the Home screen, touch-press Messages.**

   The Messages application opens. You see the message list.

2. **In the message list, press the menu key and touch-press Options.**

   The Options screen appears with two types: General Options and Email Reconciliation.

3. **Touch-press Email Reconciliation.**

   The Email Reconciliation screen opens, which has the following options:

   - *Delete On:* Configures how BlackBerry handles e-mail deletion.
   - *Wireless Reconciliation:* Turns on or off the wireless sync function.
   - *On Conflict:* Controls how BlackBerry handles any inconsistencies between e-mail on your BlackBerry and the BlackBerry Internet Service client.

   You can choose who "wins" via the Email Reconciliation option: your BlackBerry or the BlackBerry Internet Service client.

4. **For the Delete On option, touch-press one of the following:**

   - *Handheld:* A delete on your BlackBerry takes effect on your BlackBerry only.

- *Mailbox & Handheld:* A delete on your BlackBerry takes effect on both your BlackBerry and your inbox on the BlackBerry Internet Service client.

- *Prompt:* This option makes BlackBerry ask you to confirm at the time of deletion.

5. **For Wireless Reconciliation, touch-press On.**

   The changes you make on device will match the one on your e-mail account.

6. **For On Conflict, touch-press one of the following from the drop-down list.**

   - *Handheld Wins:* The e-mail messages in your e-mail account will match the ones on the handheld.

   - *Mailbox Wins:* The e-mail messages on your handheld will match the ones on your email account.

Unfortunately, some e-mail accounts might not work well with the e-mail reconciliation feature of the BlackBerry, so you might have to delete an e-mail twice.

Permanently deleting e-mail from your BlackBerry

When deleting e-mail on your BlackBerry, the same message in that e-mail account is placed in the Deleted folder. You can set up your BlackBerry to permanently delete e-mail, but use this option with caution — after that e-mail is gone, it's gone.

To permanently delete e-mail on your Service client from your BlackBerry, follow these steps:

1. **Open the Messages application.**

   The message list opens.

2. **Press the menu key and touch-press Options.**

   The Options screen opens.

3. **Touch-press E-mail Reconciliation.**

   The E-mail Reconciliation screen opens.

4. **Press the menu key and touch-press Purge Deleted Items.**

   You see a listing of all your e-mail accounts.

5. **Choose the e-mail account from which you want to purge deleted items.**

   A screen warns that you are about to purge deleted e-mails on your Service client.

6. **If you're sure you want to never see these messages again, touch-press Yes.**

   Deleted e-mails in the selected e-mail account are purged.

Unfortunately, some e-mail accounts might not work with the purge deleted items feature.

Automating replies and out-of-office messages

Unfortunately, the BlackBerry Internet Service doesn't have the "out-of-office" message feature, but that doesn't mean you can't work around it.

One way to set your out-of-office is by going to your e-mail service account (Gmail, Yahoo!, Hotmail, and so on) and set the out-of-office message from there. If you have more than one e-mail account routed to your BlackBerry, you have to do this for each. Not ideal, but it works.

Accessing Messages

From Messages, you send and receive your e-mails and also configure wireless e-mail reconciliation with your e-mail account(s).

To access Messages, touch-press the Messages icon on the Home screen.

The message list appears. Your message list can contain e-mail, voice mail messages, missed phone call notices, Short Messaging Service (SMS) messages, and even saved Web pages.

Receiving e-mails

Whether you're concerned about data security or delivery speed, with BlackBerry's up-to-date secured network, you're in good hands.

And whether you've combined accounts or use the plain-vanilla BlackBerry e-mail account, you receive your e-mail the same way. When you get an e-mail message, your BlackBerry notifies you by displaying a number next to a mail icon (an envelope) at the top of the screen. This number represents how many new, unread e-mails you have. The asterisk next to the envelope indicates new mail that you haven't opened in the Messages application.

Your BlackBerry can also notify you of new e-mail by vibration, a sound, or both. You can customize this from the Profile application as detailed in Chapter 3.

Retrieving your e-mail is simple:

1. **From the Home screen, touch-press the Messages icon.**

   Doing so allows you to view your message list.

2. **Touch-press the e-mail message you want to read.**

   You can tell whether an e-mail is unopened by the small unopened envelope icon on the left side of the e-mail. A read e-mail bears an opened envelope icon; a sent e-mail has a check mark as its icon; and a document icon represents a draft e-mail.

3. **After you finish reading the message, press the escape key to return to the message list.**

Sorting the message list

The BlackBerry lists items by the date and time you got them, but you can sort by different criteria.

On the BlackBerry, you can search your e-mail by the sender's name or by keywords. Or you could run a search as broad as looking through all the e-mail that has been sent to you. See the later section, "Searching Messages Like a Pro," for more on searching and sorting. For more predefined hot keys, see the upcoming section, "Reusing saved searches."

Saving a message to the saved folder

You can save any important e-mail in a folder so you can find it without sorting through tons of e-mail. To do so, touch-press the e-mail you want to save, press the menu key, and touch-press Save. A pop-up message confirms that your e-mail has been saved. *Note:* Your saved e-mail still remains in the message list.

To retrieve or view a saved e-mail, follow these steps:

1. **Open the Messages application.**

2. **Press the menu key and touch-press View Saved Messages.**

   You see the list of all the messages you saved.

3. **Touch-press the message you want to view.**

Viewing attachments

Your BlackBerry Storm lets you view most e-mail attachments just like you can on a desktop PC. And we're talking sizeable attachments, too, such as JPEG photo files, Word docs, PowerPoint slides, and Excel spreadsheets. Table 7-1 has a list of supported attachments viewable from your BlackBerry.

Table 7-1	BlackBerry-Supported Attachments
Supported Attachment Extension	*Description*
.bmp	BMP image file format
.doc	MS Word document
.dot	MS Word document template
.gif	GIF image file format
.htm, .html	HTML Web page
.jpg	JPEG image file format
.pdf	Adobe PDF document
.png	PNG image file format
.ppt	MS PowerPoint document
.tif	TIFF image file format
.txt	Text file
.wpd	Corel WordPerfect document
.xls	MS Excel document
.zip	Compressed file format
.wav	Music file format
.mp3	Compressed music file format

To tell whether an e-mail has an attachment, look for the standard paper clip icon next to your e-mail in the message list.

You retrieve all the different types of attachments the same way. This makes retrieving attachments an easy task. To open an attachment, follow along:

1. **With an e-mail open, press the menu key and touch-press Open Attachment.**

   You see a screen containing the name of the file, a Table of Contents option, and a Full Contents option.

   • For *Word documents,* you can see different headings in outline form in the Table of Contents option.

- For *picture files,* such as a JPEG, you can simply go straight to the Full Contents option to see the graphic.

- For *all supported file types,* you see Table of Contents and Full Contents as options. Depending on the file type, use your judgment on when you should use the Table of Contents option.

2. **Scroll to Full Contents, press the menu key, and touch-press Retrieve.**

Your BlackBerry attempts to contact the BlackBerry Internet Service client to retrieve your attachment. This retrieves only part of your attachment. BlackBerry retrieves more as you scroll through the attachment.

Editing attachments

Your BlackBerry Storm comes with Documents to Go, which means you not only can view but also edit Word and PowerPoint documents. You can even save the documents to your BlackBerry and later transfer them to your PC.

As an example, we show you how to edit a Word document attached to an e-mail:

1. **Open an e-mail.**

2. **In the message list, open an e-mail with a Word document attached.**

The e-mail opens for you to read. Notice the little paper clip, indicating that it has an attachment.

3. **Press the menu key and touch-press Open Attachment.**

You are asked if you want to view the Word document or Edit with Documents To Go.

4. **Touch-press Edit with Documents To Go.**

Here you can view your documents.

5. **Press the menu key and touch-press Edit Mode.**

With Edit Mode, you can edit your document. When you finish editing, you can save the doc on your BlackBerry Storm or e-mail it. For these steps, we e-mail it.

If you want to save the attachment on to your BlackBerry, go to the folder structure on your BlackBerry. For documents, the default folder structure is usually under Document folder.

6. **Press the menu key and touch-press Send via E-mail.**

An e-mail message opens with the Word document attached. Follow the steps in the next section to send this e-mail.

Sending e-mail

The first thing you probably want to do when you get your BlackBerry is write an e-mail to let your friends know that you've just gotten a BlackBerry.

Follow these steps:

1. **Open the Messages application.**
2. **Press the menu key and touch-press Compose Email.**

   You're prompted with a blank e-mail that you need to fill out as you would on your PC.

3. **In the To field, type the recipient's name or e-mail address.**

   As you type, you see a list of contacts from your Contacts matching the name or address that you're typing. You can make a selection from this list.

4. **Type your message subject and body.**
5. **When you're finished, press the menu key and touch-press Send.**

   Your message has wings.

Forwarding e-mail

When you need to share an important e-mail with a colleague or friend, you can forward that e-mail. Simply do the following:

1. **Open the e-mail.**
2. **Press the menu key and touch-press Forward.**
3. **Type the recipient's name or e-mail address in the appropriate space.**

   When you start typing your recipient's name, a drop-down list of your contacts appears and you can choose from it.

4. **Type a message if needed.**
5. **Press the menu key and touch-press Send.**

   Your message is on its way to your recipient.

Sending e-mail to multiple people

When you need to send an e-mail to more than one person, just keep adding recipient names as needed. You can also add recipient names to receive a CC (carbon copy) or BCC (blind carbon copy). Here's how:

1. **Open the e-mail.**

2. **Press the menu key and touch-press Compose Email.**

3. **Specify the To field for the e-mail recipient; then press the enter key.**

    Another To field is added below the first. The CC field works the same way.

4. **To add a BCC recipient, press the menu key and touch-press Add BCC.**

    You see a BCC field. You can specify a blind carbon-copy (BCC) recipient the same way you do To and CC recipients.

Whether you're writing a new e-mail, replying, or forwarding an e-mail, the way you add new CC and BCC fields is the same.

Saving a draft e-mail

Sometimes the most skillful wordsmiths find themselves lacking. Don't fret, fellow wordsmith; you can save that e-mail as a draft until your words come to you. Just press the menu key and touch-press Save Draft.

Your e-mail is saved as a draft. When you're ready to send your message, choose the draft from the message list. You can tell which messages are drafts because they sport a tiny document icon; finished messages have an envelope icon.

Attaching any file to your e-mail

Many people are surprised that you can attach any document on your BlackBerry Storm or in the microSD card (in your Storm). When we say *any* file type, we mean Word, Excel, PowerPoint documents, as well as pictures, music, videos.

1. **Open the Messages application.**

2. **Press the menu key and touch-press Compose.**

    You're prompted with a blank e-mail.

3. **In the To field, type the recipient's name or e-mail address.**

    As you type, you see a list of contacts from your Contacts matching the name or address that you're typing. You can make a selection from this list.

4. **Type your message subject and body.**

5. **Press the menu key and touch-press Attach File.**

You're prompted with folders. Think of them as the folders on your PC.

6. **Touch-press the folders until you get to the file you want to send; touch-press that file.**

   You see the file in the e-mail message.

7. **Press the menu key and touch-press Send.**

   Your message has wings.

Spell checking your outgoing messages

Whether you're composing an e-mail message or an SMS text message (see Chapter 8), you can always check your spelling with the built-in spell checker. Simply press the menu key and touch-press Check Spelling.

When it finds an error, the BlackBerry spell checker makes a suggestion, as shown in Figure 7-3. If you want to skip that word and go on to the next, press the escape key. If you want to skip spell checking altogether for an e-mail, press and hold the escape key.

If you're used to MS Word dot-underlining a misspelled word, your BlackBerry Storm does the same.

Figure 7-3:
The
BlackBerry
spell
checker is
in action.

By default, the spell checker doesn't kick in before you send your message, but you can change that:

1. **Open the Messages application.**

2. **Press the menu key and touch-press Options.**

3. **Touch-press Spell Check.**

4. **Make sure Spell Check E-mail Before Sending is checked.**

5. **Press the menu key and touch-press Save.**

Adding a sender to your Contacts

You can add a message sender's contact info to your BlackBerry Contacts directly from Messages. You don't even have to copy or write down the person's name and e-mail address on paper.

To add a sender to your Contacts, follow these steps:

1. **From the Home screen, press the menu key and touch-press Messages.**

2. **Touch-press the e-mail whose sender you want added to your Contacts.**

3. **From the opened e-mail, scroll to the sender's name, press the menu key, and then touch-press Add to Contacts.**

   The New Contacts screen opens. The sender's first name, last name, and e-mail address are transferred automatically to your Contacts.

4. **If needed, add information (such as phone number and mailing address).**

5. **Press the menu key and touch-press Save.**

Deleting e-mail

Keeping your message list tidy can help you stay organized and reduce the amount of memory your e-mail takes.

Cull those messages you no longer need by following these steps:

1. **From the Home screen, touch-press Messages.**

2. **Highlight the e-mail you want to delete and press the Delete key.**

   A deletion confirmation screen appears.

3. **Touch-press Delete to confirm your deletion.**

   The deleted e-mail is toast.

To delete more than one e-mail, press the cap key and scroll to highlight as many e-mails as you want. After you make your deletion selections, press the Delete key.

You can delete anything listed in the message list (such as an SMS or a voice mail) the same way you delete an e-mail message.

If you want to really clean up your old e-mails and don't want to scroll through tons of messages, you can do the following:

1. **Open the Messages application.**

2. **Highlight a horizontal date mark, press the menu key, and touch-press Delete Prior.**

   The *date mark* is simply a horizontal bar with dates. Just like you can highlight e-mails in the message list, you can also highlight the date mark.

   A pop-up prompts you for delete confirmation. Before you take the plunge, remember that going ahead will *delete all the e-mails before the particular date mark.* There is no way to retrieve deleted items from your BlackBerry.

3. **Touch-press Delete to confirm your deletion.**

   All your e-mails prior to the date mark are history.

Filtering your e-mail

Most of your e-mail isn't urgent (and sometimes doesn't really concern you). Instead of receiving them on your BlackBerry — and wasting both time and effort — filter them out. While in the BlackBerry Internet Service client, set up filters to make your BlackBerry mailbox receive only those e-mails that you care about. (Don't worry; you'll still receive them on your main computer.)

This example creates a simple filter that treats work-related messages as urgent and forwards them to your BlackBerry. Follow these steps:

1. **Log into the BlackBerry Internet Service client.**

   Refer to Figure 7-1.

2. **Click the Filter icon for the desired e-mail account.**

   The Filter screen shows a list of filters that have been created. See Figure 7-4.

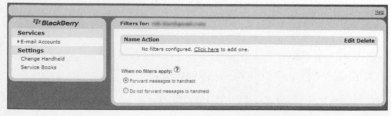

Figure 7-4:
Filter list
screen.

3. **Click the Click Here link.**

   The Add Filter screen appears, as shown in Figure 7-5.

Figure 7-5:
Create a fil-
ter for your
e-mail here.

4. **Enter a filter name.**

   The filter name can be anything you like. We entered WorkUrgent.

5. **In the Apply Filter When drop-down list, choose the condition to place on the filter:**

   - *A High-Priority Mail Arrives:* Select this option if the filter applies only to urgent e-mail.

   - *Subject Field Contains:* When selected, the Contains field is enabled; you can type text in it. Specify what keywords the filter will look for in the subject field. Separate each entry with a semicolon (;).

   - *From Field Contains:* When selected, the Contains field is enabled; you can type text in it. Type a full or part of an address. For example, you can type *rob@robkao.com* or just *kao*. Separate each entry with a semicolon (;).

   - *To Field Contains:* Similar to From Field Contains.

   - *CC Field Contains:* Similar to From Field Contains.

   This example selects From Field Contains.

6. **Specify the text in the Contains field.**

   See details in the preceding step for what to enter in the Contains field. This example types the domain of your work e-mail address. For example, if your work e-mail address is myName@XYZCo.com, enter **XYZCo.com**.

7. **Select one of the following options:**

   Forward Messages to Handheld: You can select either or both of the following two check boxes:

- *Header Only:* Choose this if you want only the header of the e-mails that meets the condition(s) you set in Steps 3–5 to be sent to you. (A *header* doesn't contain the message — just who sent it, the subject, and the time it was sent.) Choose this if you get automated alerts, where receiving only the subject is sufficient.

- *Level 1 Notification:* Level1 notification is another way of saying *urgent e-mail.* A Level1 e-mail is bold in Messages.

Do Not Forward Message to Handheld: Any e-mail that meets the conditions you set in Steps 3–5 doesn't go to your BlackBerry.

8. **Confirm your filter by clicking the Add Filter button.**

You return to the Filter screen, where you can see your newly created filter in the list.

If you have a hard time setting the criteria for a filter, guesstimate and then check it by having a friend send you a test e-mail. If the test e-mail isn't filtered correctly, set the conditions until you get them right.

Searching Messages Like a Pro

Searching is one of those functions you probably won't use every day — but when you do run a search, you usually need the information fast. Take a few minutes here to familiarize yourself with general searching.

The BlackBerry Messages application provides three ways to search through your messages. Two of the three ways are specific, and one is a broad search:

- ✔ **Search by sender or recipient:** Specific. This method assumes that you already know the sender or recipient.

- ✔ **Search by subject:** Specific. This approach assumes that you already know the subject.

- ✔ **General search:** Broad. You don't have a specific assumption.

You can search through anything listed in the messages list. This means you can search through SMS and voice mail as well as e-mail.

Searching by sender or recipient

Search by sender or recipient when you're looking for a specific message from a specific person. For example, suppose your brother constantly sends you e-mail (which means your message list has many entries from him). You're trying to locate a message he sent you about two weeks ago regarding a fishing trip location. You've scrolled down the message list, but you just can't find that message.

To find a message when you know the sender or recipient, follow these steps:

1. **Open the Messages application.**
2. **Highlight a message that you sent to or received from that particular person.**

    The choice you get in the next step depends on whether you highlighted a sent message or a received message.

3. **Press the menu key and touch-press one of these options:**

    - *From Someone Specific:* Because that certain someone sent you the message, choose Search Sender.

    - *To Someone Specific:* Because you sent that certain someone the message, choose Search Recipient.

    The search starts. Any results appear onscreen.

Searching by subject

Search by subject when you're looking for a specifically titled e-mail. As when you're searching by sender or recipient, first scroll to an e-mail bearing the same subject you're searching for. Then follow these steps:

1. **Open the Messages application.**
2. **Highlight an e-mail titled by the subject you're searching for.**
3. **Press the menu key and touch-press Search Subject.**

    The search starts, and the results appear onscreen.

Running a general search

A general search is a broad search from which you can perform keyword searches of your messages. To run a general search:

1. **Open the Messages application.**

2. **Press the menu key and touch-press Search.**

   The Search screen appears.

3. **Fill in your search criteria; see Figure 7-6.**

   The criteria for a general search follow:

   - *Name:* This is the name of the sender or recipient to search by.

   - *In:* This is related to Name. Use this menu to indicate where the name might appear. Your choices are From, To, Cc, Bcc, and any address field.

   - *Subject:* This is where you type some or all the keywords that appear in the subject.

   - *Message:* Enter keywords that appear in the message.

   - *Service:* If you set up your BlackBerry to receive e-mail from more than one e-mail account, you can specify which e-mail account to search.

   - *Folder:* This is the folder you want to look in. Generally, you should search all folders.

   - *Show:* This list specifies how the search result will appear (namely, whether you want to see only e-mails that you sent or e-mails that you received). Your choices are Sent and Received, Received Only, Sent Only, Saved Only, Draft Only, and Unopened Only.

   - *Type:* This list specifies the type of message you're trying to search for. Your choices are All, E-mail, E-mail with Attachments, PIN, SMS, Phone, and Voice Mail.

   From the Search screen shown in Figure 7-6, you can have multiple search criteria or just a single one; it's up to you.

4. **Press the menu key and touch-press Search to launch your search.**

   The search results appear onscreen.

Figure 7-6:
The Search
screen in
Messages.

You can narrow the search results by performing a second search on the initial results. For example, you can search by sender and then narrow those results by performing a second search by subject.

You can also search by sender or recipient when you're looking for a specific message from a specific person. To do so, scroll to an e-mail bearing the specific sender or recipient. Press the menu key and touch-press Search Sender or Search Recipient. If the e-mail that you highlighted is an incoming e-mail, you'll see Search Sender. If the e-mail is outgoing, you'll see Search Recipient.

Saving search results

If you find yourself re-searching with the same criteria over and over, you might want to save the search and then reuse it. Here's how:

1. **Open the Messages application.**

2. **Press the menu key and touch-press Search.**

   The Search screen appears.

 3. **Fill in your search criteria.**

 Refer to the "Running a general search" section in this chapter for option explanations.

 4. **Press the menu key and touch-press Save.**

 The Save Search screen appears, from which you can name your search and assign it a shortcut key. See Figure 7-7.

Figure 7-7:
Name your search and assign it a shortcut key.

 5. **In the Title field, enter a name.**

 The title is the name of your search, which appears in the Search Result screen.

 6. **Touch-press the Shortcut Key field, and then touch-press a letter from the drop-down list.**

 You have 20-plus letters to choose from.

 7. **Confirm your saved search by pressing the menu key and touch-pressing Save.**

Reusing saved searches

Your BlackBerry comes with five saved search results. Any new saved result makes your search that much more robust.

You can see all saved search results:

1. **Open the Messages application.**

2. **Press the menu key and touch-press Search.**

3. **Press the menu key and touch-press Recall.**

   The recall screen opens, and you can see the five preloaded search shortcuts, as shown in Figure 7-8.

To reuse one of the saved search results, choose a search from the list (shown in Figure 7-8), press the menu key, and touch-press Search.

If you have multiple accounts, set up a search shortcut so you view one specific account when you want to (for example, you have Gmail for personal and your small business e-mail account both set up on your BlackBerry). You see e-mail from both in the Messages application, which can be overwhelming. From the General Search screen, set the Service criteria to the one you want, and follow the steps to save the search and assign a shortcut key. The next time you want to see one account, you can get to it in an instance!

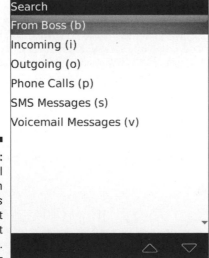

Figure 7-8:
The recall
screen
shows
default
search hot
keys.

Long Live E-Mail

No closet has unlimited space, and your BlackBerry e-mail storage has limits, too. You've likely pondered how long your e-mails are kept in your BlackBerry. (The default is 30 days. Pshew.)

You can choose several options: from 15 days to forever, and because your BlackBerry Storm comes with 1GB of internal memory, it should last you a while!

Because any message you save is kept for as long as you want, saving a message is a good way to make sure you don't lose an important message.

To change how long your e-mails live on your BlackBerry, follow these steps:

1. **Open the Messages application.**

2. **Press the menu key and touch-press Options.**

3. **Touch-press General Options.**

4. **Touch-press Keep Messages and then touch-press Forever.**

    • *Forever:* If you choose Forever, you'll seldom need to worry about your e-mails being automatically deleted.

    A good way to archive your e-mail is to back up your e-mails by using BlackBerry Desktop Manager. See Chapter 16 for more on backing up your BlackBerry on your PC.

    • *Time Option:* If you choose a set time option, any message older than that time frame is automatically deleted from your BlackBerry the next time you reboot your BlackBerry. However, it will be deleted only on your BlackBerry — even if you turn on e-mail reconciliation — because these deletions are not completed manually by you.

5. **Confirm your changes by pressing the menu key and touch-pressing Save.**

Chapter 8

Too Cool for E-Mail

*Y*our BlackBerry Storm is primarily a communication tool, with e-mail as a major driver. It's a wonderful technology, but you might find yourself in a situation where other means of communication are more appropriate. For instance, e-mail isn't the tool of choice for instant messaging — most people would find that method slow and cumbersome. Nor is e-mail the best tool to use when you want to alert someone to something.

Your BlackBerry offers some less obvious ways to communicate — ways that might serve as the perfect fit for a special situation. Here you get the inside scoop on PIN-to-PIN messaging and text messaging (also known as *Short Messaging Service,* or *SMS*). We also give you tips on how to turn your BlackBerry into a lean (and not-so-mean) instant messaging (IM) machine.

Sending and Receiving PIN-to-PIN Messages

What happens when you use PIN-to-PIN messaging? First and foremost, we'll get the acronym out of the way. *PIN* stands for *personal identification number* (familiar to anyone who's ever used an ATM) and uniquely identifies your device.

PIN-to-PIN, then, is another way of saying *one BlackBerry to another BlackBerry.*

As for the other details, they're straightforward. PIN-to-PIN messaging is based on the technology underpinning two-way pager systems. Unlike sending a standard e-mail, when you send a PIN-to-PIN message, the message doesn't venture outside RIM's infrastructure in search of an e-mail server and (eventually) an e-mail inbox. Instead, it stays solidly in the RIM (Research In Motion) world, where it's shunted through the recipient's network provider until it ends up on the recipient's BlackBerry.

Here's the neat part. According to RIM, the message isn't saved anywhere in this universe *except* on the one device that sends the PIN message and the other device that receives it. Compare that with an e-mail, which is saved in at least four separate locations (the mail client and e-mail servers of both sender and recipient) not to mention all the system's redundancies and backups. Think of it this way: If you whisper a little secret in someone's ear, only you and that special someone know what was said. In a way, PIN-to-PIN messaging is the same thing, with one BlackBerry whispering to another BlackBerry. Now that's discreet.

If you tend to read the financial newspapers — especially those that cover corporate lawsuits extensively — you know that there's no such thing as private e-mail. PIN-to-PIN messaging — in theory at least — is as good as the old Code of Silence. Now, is such privacy really an advantage? You can argue both sides of the issue, depending on what you want to use PIN-to-PIN messaging for.

Basically, if you like the idea that your communications can be kept discreet, PIN-to-PIN messaging has great curb appeal. If you don't care about privacy issues, though, you still might be impressed by PIN-to-PIN messaging's zippy nature. (It really is the Ferrari of wireless communication — way faster than e-mail.)

Getting a BlackBerry PIN

When you try to call somebody on the telephone, you can't get far without a telephone number. As you might expect, the same principle applies to PIN-to-PIN messaging: no PIN, no PIN-to-PIN messaging.

In practical terms, you need the PIN of any BlackBerry you want to send a PIN message. (You also need to find your own PIN so you can hand it out to those folks who want to message you.)

The cautious side of you might be wondering why on earth you'd give your PIN to somebody. This PIN isn't the same as your password. In fact, this PIN doesn't give anybody access to your BlackBerry or do anything to compromise security. It's simply an identification; you treat it the same way you treat your phone number.

A little bit of RIM history

Sometime during the last millennium, Research In Motion (RIM) wasn't even in the phone business. Before BlackBerry became all the rage with SmartPhone features, RIM was doing a tidy little business with its wireless e-mail. Back then, RIM's primitive wireless e-mail service was served by network service providers on a radio bandwidth, namely DataTAC and Mobitex networks. These were separate from a typical cellphone infrastructure's bandwidth. RIM devices at that time already had PIN-to-PIN messaging. This type of messaging is akin to a pager, where a message doesn't live in a mailbox but is sent directly to the BlackBerry without any delay. (No one wants a paging system

that moves at turtle speed when you can get one that moves like a jack rabbit, right?)

Several interesting facts followed from RIM's initial decision. Of note, most cellphone users in New York City were left without service during the 9/11 disaster. As you can understand, the entire cellphone infrastructure in New York and surrounding areas was overwhelmed when faced with too many people trying to use the bandwidth available. However, one communication device continued to work during that stressful time — RIM's PIN-to-PIN messaging kept the information flow going.

RIM makes getting hold of a PIN easy. In fact, you get two quick paths to PIN enlightenment:

✔ **From the Message screen:** Send your PIN from the Message screen with the help of a *keyword.* When you type a preset word, your BlackBerry replaces what you type with a bit of information specific to your device. Sound wacky? It's actually easier than it sounds.

To see what we mean, just compose a new message. (Chapter 7 gives you the basics on the whole e-mail message and messaging thing, if you need a refresher.) In the subject or body of your message, type **mypin** and add a space. As soon as you type the space, `mypin` is miraculously transformed into your PIN in the format `pin:your-pin-number`, as shown in Figure 8-1. Isn't that neat? *Note:* Case doesn't matter here.

`mypin` isn't the only keyword that RIM predefines for you. You can try `mynumber` for your phone number and `myver` for the OS version of your Storm.

✔ **From the Status screen:** Most BlackBerry models display the Status screen when you touch-press in succession the following links starting from the Home screen: menu, Options, and Status. Figure 8-2 shows a typical Status screen. (The PIN is fourth on the list of items shown.)

To:
Cc:
Subject:
Mypin
1 .,!? 2 ABC 3 DEF
4 GHI 5 JKL 6 MNO
7 PQRS 8 TUV 9 WXYZ
* :;() 0 space # aA
!?123 sym
To:
Cc:
Subject:
pin:2100000A
1 .,!? 2 ABC 3 DEF
4 GHI 5 JKL 6 MNO
7 PQRS 8 TUV 9 WXYZ
* :;() 0 space # aA
!?123 sym

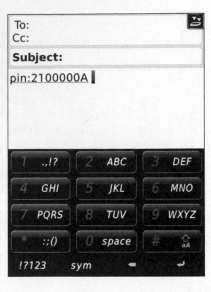

Figure 8-1: Type a keyword (left), add a space, and see it get translated (right).

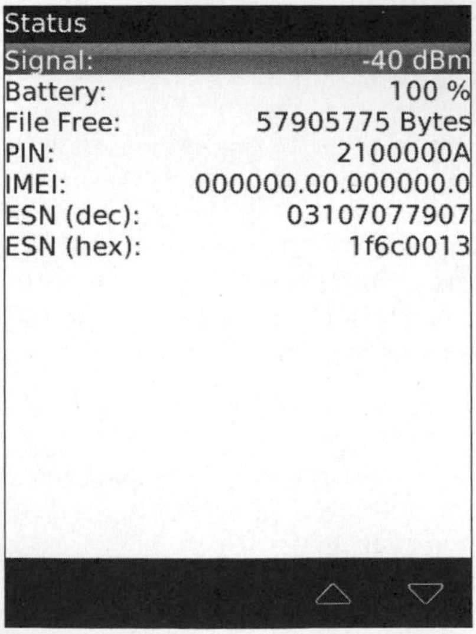

Status
Signal: -40 dBm
Battery: 100 %
File Free: 57905775 Bytes
PIN: 2100000A
IMEI: 000000.00.000000.0
ESN (dec): 03107077907
ESN (hex): 1f6c0013

Figure 8-2: Find your PIN on the Status screen.

Assigning PINs to names

So, you convince your BlackBerry-wielding buddies to go to the trouble of finding out their PINs and passing said PINs to you. Now the trick is finding a convenient place to store your PINs so you can use them. Luckily for you, you have an obvious choice: BlackBerry Contacts. And RIM, in its infinite wisdom, makes storing such info a snap. To add a PIN to someone's contact info in Contacts, do the following:

1. **From the Home screen, touch-press Contacts.**

   Contacts opens.

2. **Highlight a contact name; press the menu key.**

3. **Touch-press Edit.**

   The Edit Contact screen appears.

4. **Scroll down to the PIN field, as shown in Figure 8-3.**

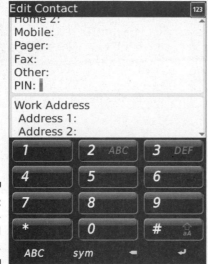

Figure 8-3:
Add a con-
tact's PIN
info here.

5. **Type the PIN.**

6. **Press the menu key.**

7. **Touch-press Save.**

   It's that simple. Of course, it's even easier if you think ahead and enter
   the PIN information you have when you set up your initial contact info
   (by using the New Address screen), but we understand that a PIN isn't
   the kind of information people carry around.

If all this talk about New Address screens and Edit Address screens doesn't
sound familiar, check out Chapter 4, which covers the Contacts application in
more detail.

Sending a PIN-to-PIN message

PIN-to-PIN means *from one BlackBerry to another.*

Sending a PIN-to-PIN message is no different than sending an e-mail. Follow these steps if you have a contact's PIN stored in Contacts:

1. **From the Home screen, touch-press Contacts.**

   Contacts opens.

2. **Touch-press a contact name and press the menu key.**

   If a contact has a PIN, you see a menu item titled `PIN <contact name>`. Say you have a contact named Rob Kao. When you touch-press his name in the list and press the menu key, `PIN Rob Kao` appears as a menu option, as shown in Figure 8-4.

3. **Touch-press PIN *<contact name>* from the menu.**

   The New Message screen appears, with your buddy's PIN already entered.

4. **Enter the rest of the text boxes — subject, message body, and signoff — just as you would an e-mail.**

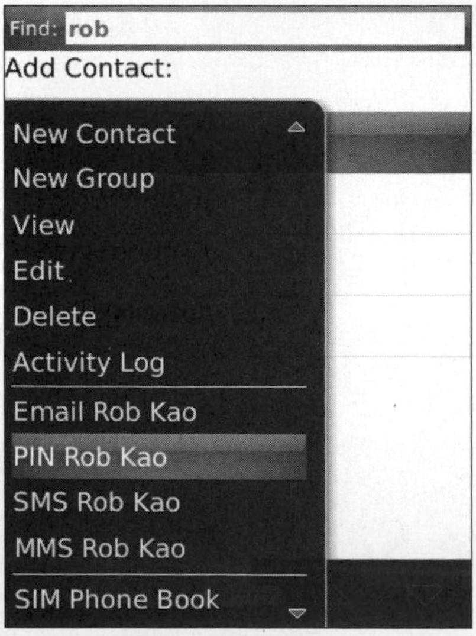

Find: **rob**

Add Contact:

New Contact
New Group
View
Edit
Delete
Activity Log
Email Rob Kao
PIN Rob Kao
SMS Rob Kao
MMS Rob Kao
SIM Phone Book

Figure 8-4:
Send a PIN
message
via your
Contacts.

Alternatively, if you know the PIN, you can also type it directly. Here's how:

1. **From the Home screen, touch-press Messages.**

   The Messages application opens.

2. **Press the menu key.**

3. **Touch-press Compose PIN.**

   The ever-familiar New Message screen makes an appearance.

4. **Type the PIN in the To field.**

5. **Add a subject, the message, and sign off just like you would in an e-mail.**

Because of the nature of PIN-to-PIN messaging (the conspicuous lack of a paper trail, as it were), companies can disable PIN-to-PIN messaging on your BlackBerry device. (No paper trail can mean legal problems down the road — can you say *Sarbanes-Oxley?*)

If your BlackBerry is from your employer and you don't see the PIN menu item, you can safely assume that your employer has disabled it. Contact your *BlackBerry Enterprise Server (BES)* administrator to make sure. Keep in mind that even if your company has disabled PIN-to-PIN messaging, folks can still PIN you — you just can't PIN them back.

Receiving a PIN-to-PIN message

Receiving a PIN-to-PIN message is no different than receiving a standard e-mail. You get the same entry in your Messages list for the PIN-to-PIN message, and the same screen appears when you open the message.

By default, your BlackBerry vibrates to alert you, but you can change this in Profiles (check Chapter 3 for more details on changing your profile). When you reply to the message, the reply is a PIN-to-PIN message as well — that is, as long as your BlackBerry is set up to send PIN-to-PIN messages. Otherwise, you can't reply, period.

Regardless of whether your BlackBerry is enabled for sending PIN-to-PIN messages, you can always receive a PIN message. BES administrators can mandate that you can't send PIN messages, but that can't stop you from receiving them.

Keeping in Touch the SMS/MMS Way

Short Messaging Service (also known as *SMS* or *text messaging*) is so popular these days that you can vote that way — for an *American Idol,* anyway. *Multimedia Messaging Service (MMS)* is the latest evolution of SMS. Rather than a simple text message, you can also send an audio or video clip.

How short is *short?* The maximum size per message is about 160 characters. If you send more than that, it gets broken down into multiple messages.

SMS is a smash!

In the early days of SMS, phone providers gave away their text messaging services for free. It caught on like wildfire, especially in developing countries where folks are a tad more cost-conscious. In those countries, it didn't take long before lots of folks started carrying a cellphone just to avail themselves of the free text messaging. Adding to the appeal was the fact that many network service providers didn't even force you to pay for a plan; you could walk into any convenience store and buy a prepaid *Subscriber Identification Module (SIM)* card, no questions asked.

In the United States, however, it took some time for SMS to catch up. For one thing, network service providers in the U.S. are divided between CDMA and GSM/GPRS technology. (See Chapter 1 for more on that divide.) GSM/GPRS phones have allowed for SMS since 1991; CDMA phones didn't until about 2000. (Competing innovations do have a downside, right?) The second reason is that most U.S. homes are wired for regular phone service, so cellphones aren't necessarily seen as something you just gotta have. Eventually, though, the convenience of using cellphones will make them more and more attractive — and, of course, SMS is the next logical step.

Moreover, SMS is an established technology (not a new and unproven thing, in other words) that's been popular for years in Europe and Asia.

Text messaging does pose a challenge for beginners. It isn't tough; it's just cumbersome to type the letters by using the size of virtual keypad. Also, you need to know the trends and options for text messaging. In-the-know folks use abbreviations that might be difficult for you to understand in the beginning, so don't dive in without your oxygen tank.

A quick preparation goes a long way toward avoiding being labeled *uncool* when it comes to your SMS syntax. The upcoming sections help smooth your path a bit by filling you in on the basics of SMS-speak.

Using shorthand for speedy replies

On a regular cellphone, three letters share one key. As you can imagine, trying to bang out even a single paragraph can be a real pain.

Human ingenuity prevails. Abbreviations cut down on the amount you need to enter. This *texting* (short for text messaging) language is quite hip, especially among the 14–18-year-old set. Veteran text messagers (the hip ones, at least) can easily spot someone who's new to SMS technology by how they don't use the right lingo (or use such lingo incorrectly).

SMS beginners might be tempted to rely on BlackBerry's default SureType feature when texting. *SureType* is a technology used initially in BlackBerry 7100 series and carried on in the BlackBerry Storm. SureType compensates for the limited keys when you hold your BlackBerry up-and-down (portrait mode). The software is smart enough to predict what you want to type. It also can become smarter as you use it. The technology lets you type words faster and more easily on the portrait mode. However, you might get texts from buddies who use cool, with-it, hip, shorthand lingo, and you respond with uncool, without-it, lame, complete words provided for you by SureType technology.

To preserve (or create) your cool image, hold your Storm lengthwise (landscape) and you get a full QWERTY keyboard, which means SureType is disabled.

Awhfy?

When texting, you want to craft a sentence with as few letters as possible. Because texting has been around for years, plenty of folks have risen to this challenge by coming up with a considerable pool of useful abbreviations. Don't feel you have to rush out and memorize the whole shorthand dictionary at once, though.

As with mastering a new language, start out with the most commonly used words or sentences. Then when you become familiar with those, slowly gather in more and more terms. In time, the whole shorthand thing will be second nature.

And what are the most commonly used terms out there? Funny you should ask. Table 8-1 gives our take on the most common abbreviations, which are enough to get you started. With these under your belt, you can at least follow the most important parts of an SMS conversation. Feel free to check out the Web site associated with this book (www.blackberryfordummies.com) for a more comprehensive list of shorthand abbreviations.

Showing some emotion

Written words have gotten folks into trouble now and then; the very same words can mean different things to different people. A simple example is the phrase, "You're clueless." When you speak such a phrase (with the appropriate facial and hand gestures), your friend knows (we hope) that you're teasing and that it's all a bit of fun. Write that same phrase in a text message and, well, you might get a nasty reply in return — which you then have to respond to, which prompts another response, and soon enough you've just ended a seven-year friendship.

SMS is akin to chatting, so *emoticons* show what you meant when you wrote "You're clueless." (I'm joking! I'm happy! I'm mad!) These cutesy codes let you telegraph your meaning in sledgehammer-to-the-forehead fashion.

Table 8-1		SMS Shorthand	
Shorthand	*Meaning*	*Shorthand*	*Meaning*
2D4	To die for	CUL8R	See you later
2G4U	Too good for you	CUS	See you soon
2L8	Too late	F2F	Face to face
4E	Forever	FC	Fingers crossed
4YEO	For your eyes only	FCFS	First come, first served
A3	Anytime, anywhere, anyplace	FOAF	Friend of a friend
AFAIK	As far as I know	FWIW	For what it's worth
ASAP	As soon as possible	GAL	Get a life
ASL	Age, sex, location	GG	Good game
ATM	At the moment	GR8	Great
ATW	At the weekend	GSOH	Good sense of humor
AWHFY	Are we having fun yet?	H2CUS	Hope to see you soon
B4	Before	IC	I see
BBFN	Bye-bye for now	IDK	I don't know
BBL	Be back later	IMHO	In my honest opinion
BBS	Be back soon	IMO	In my opinion
BCNU	Be seeing you	IOU	I owe you
BG	Big grin	IOW	In other words
BION	Believe it or not	KISS	Keep it simple, stupid
BOL	Best of luck	LOL	Laughing out loud
BOT	Back on topic	OIC	Oh, I see
BRB	Be right back	RUOK	Are you okay?
BRT	Be right there	W4U	Waiting for you
BTW	By the way	W8	Wait
CMON	Come on	WTG	Way to go
CU	See you	TMOZ	Tomorrow

We're talking *smileys* — those combinations of keyboard characters
that, when artfully combined, resemble a human face. The most popular
example — one that you've probably encountered in e-mails from especially
chirpy individuals — is the happy face, which (usually at the end of a
statement) conveys good intentions or a happy context, like this :). (Turn
the top of your head to the left to see the face.)

Table 8-2 shows you the range of smiley choices. Just remember that smileys
are supposed to be fun. They could be the one thing you need to make sure
that your gently teasing remark isn't seen as a hateful comment. Smileys
help, but if you aren't sure if what you're about to send can be misconstrued
even with the help of the smileys, just don't send it.

Table 8-2	Smileys and Their Meanings		
Smiley	*Meaning*	*Smiley*	*Meaning*
:)	Happy, smiling	:(	Sad, frown
:-)	Happy, smiling, with nose	:-(	Sad, frown, with nose
:D	Laughing	:-<	Super sad
:-D	Laughing, with nose	:'-(	Crying
:'-)	Tears due to laughter	:-0	Yell, gasped
:-)8	Smiling with bow tie	:-@	Scream, what?
;)	Winking	:-(o)	Shouting
;-)	Winking, with nose	|-0	Yawn
0:-)	I'm an angel (male)	:----(	Liar, long nose
0*-)	I'm an angel (female)	%-(	Confused
8-)	Cool, with sunglasses	:-|	Determined
:-!	Foot in mouth	:-()	Talking
>-)	Evil grin	:-ozz	Bored
:-x	Kiss on the lips	@@	Eyes
(((H)))	Hugs	%-)	Cross-eyed
@>--;--	Rose	|@@|	Face
:b	Tongue out	#:-)	Hair is a mess
;b	Tongue out with a wink	&:-)	Hair is curly
:-&	Tongue tied	$-)	Yuppie
-!-	Sleepy	:-($)	Put your money where your mouth is
<3	For heart or love	<(^(oo)^)>	Pig

Sending a text message

After you have the shorthand stuff and smileys under control, get your fingers pumped up and ready for action: It's message sending time! Whether it's SMS or MMS, here's how it's done:

1. **From the Home screen, touch-press Contacts.**

   The Contacts opens.

2. **Touch-press a contact that has a mobile phone number.**

   SMS only works on mobile phones.

3. **Press the menu key.**

   A menu appears.

4. **Touch-press SMS (or MMS)** *<contact name>*.

   The menu item for SMS or MMS displays the name. For example, if you choose John Doe, the menu item reads SMS John Doe or MMS John Doe, as shown in Figure 8-5. (Note the space right underneath the screen heading for entering your text message.)

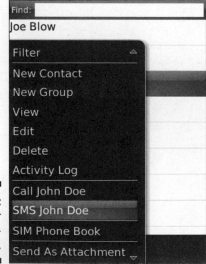

Figure 8-5:
Start your
text mes-
sage here.

5. **If you chose MMS, browse from your multimedia folders and touch-press the file you want to send.**

This extra step lets you choose the multimedia file. This is the only difference between SMS and MMS with regards to sending a message.

6. **Type your message.**

   Remember that shorthand business? You should start taking advantage of it the first chance you get. Practice makes perfect.

7. **Press the menu key.**

   A menu appears.

8. **Touch-press Send.**

   Your message is sent on its merry way.

Viewing a message

If you have an incoming SMS or MMS message, you get notified. The e-mail icon on the top of the Home screen indicates a new message. In fact, everything about viewing SMS and MMS messages is pretty much the same as reading e-mail. The basic run-through is as follows:

1. **Touch-press Messages from Home screen.**

2. **Touch-press the unread message.**

   Bob's your uncle: The message appears onscreen.

You can customize how BlackBerry tells you that you have a message. Chapter 3 has the scoop on customizing your BlackBerry, including SMS notification. (Look for the section about customizing your profile.)

You can tell your BlackBerry to separate SMS from e-mails.

1. **Touch-press Messages from Home screen.**

2. **Press the menu key.**

3. **Touch-press Options.**

4. **Touch-press General Options.**

5. **Touch-press SMS and Email Inboxes selections.**

6. **Touch-press Separate.**

7. **Press the escape key and touch-press Save.**

   An icon for SMS appears on the home screen.

Messaging — Instantly

Real-time (as they happen) conversations with your friends over the Internet are easier with *Instant Messenger (IM)*. IM allows two or more people to send and receive messages over the Internet. It all started with pure text messages and evolved into a rich medium involving voice and even video conversation in real time.

IM may not be in your BlackBerry Storm. The service provider chooses whether to include it. (Most providers, however, do *support* it for the BlackBerry Storm.) You can add Instant Messenger to your BlackBerry even if it didn't come with it. Open your browser, go to `http://mobile.black berry.com`, and navigate to the following pages in sequence: Applications and Staying in Touch. On this page, you see a download link to BlackBerry Messenger.

Messaging etiquette and a few words of caution

Here are some commonsense messaging rules as well as a few words of caution. Being new to messaging doesn't give you license to act like a jerk. Play nice and take the following pointers to heart:

✔ **Use smileys to avoid misunderstandings.** Read more about emoticons and smileys earlier in this chapter.

✔ **Don't ever forward chain letters.** We mean it. Never.

✔ **If you need to forward a message, check the entire message first.** Make sure nothing offends the recipient.

✔ **Some things in this world need to be said face-to-face, so don't even think of texting sensitive issues.** Ever try dumping your girlfriend or boyfriend over the phone? Guess what. Using messaging is far worse.

✔ **Keep your tone gender neutral.** Some messages that are forwarded through e-mails are inappropriate to the opposite sex.

✔ **All-capital letters are like shouting.** So DON'T USE THEM.

✔ **Know your recipient.** A newbie may not know smileys and shorthand, so act accordingly. (Read more about shorthand earlier in this chapter.)

✔ **Don't reply to any message when you're angry.** You can't unsend a sent message. Better to be prudent than sorry.

✔ **Don't gossip or be rude.** Beware! Your messages can end up in the wrong hands and haunt you in the future.

✔ **Easy does it.** No documented evidence reveals the deleterious effects (physical or psychological) of too much texting. However, don't text as if you want to enter the books as the first recorded case of Instantmesssagingitis. As your great-grandma would tell you, too much of anything is bad for you. It's easy to lose track of time when IMing.

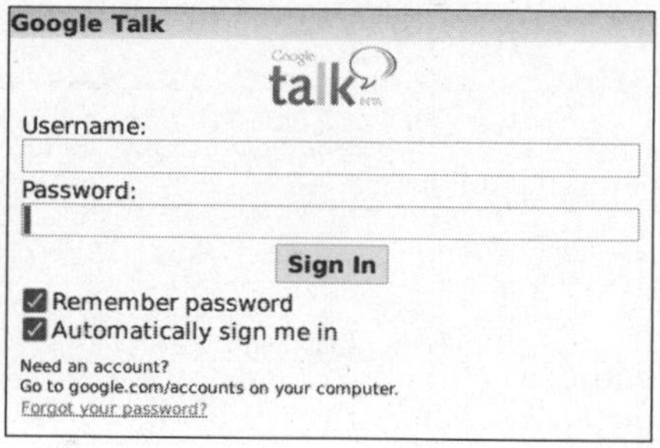

Google Talk

talk

Username:

Password:

Sign In

☑ Remember password
☑ Automatically sign me in

Need an account?
Go to google.com/accounts on your computer.
Forgot your password?

Figure 8-6:
Login
screen for
Google Talk.

We recommend enabling Save Password to save time but also set your handheld password to Enabled so you're not compromising security. Refer to Chapter 3 if you need a refresher on how to enable passwords on your BlackBerry.

The Auto Sign In check box turns on and off automatic sign-in when your BlackBerry Storm is powered up. Auto Sign In is helpful if you have a habit of turning off your BlackBerry periodically.

4. **Press the menu key and touch-press Sign In.**

   Google Talk tries to log you in and displays `Signing in you're your_loging_id`. After you're logged in, your contacts *(buddies)*, appear on the screen.

5. **Touch-press the person you want to chat with.**

   A menu appears, listing various things you can do. Features could differ a little bit for each IM application, but for Google Talk, here's a list of what you can do:

   - Start Chat
   - Send File
   - Add a Friend
   - Rename
   - Remove
   - Block

6. **Touch-press the action you want.**

Adding a contact/buddy

Before you can start chatting with your buddies, you need to know their user IDs as well. Table 8-3 shows how you can obtain user IDs from the various messenger services.

Table 8-3	Finding User IDs
Provider	*Where You Get Someone's User ID*
AIM	Your friend or search AOL's directory
Google Talk	The text before the @ sign in his Google e-mail address
Yahoo!	Text before the @ sign in his Yahoo! e-mail address
ICQ	Your friend's e-mail or the ICQ Global Directory
MSN	MSN passport ID or Hotmail ID

Luckily for you, you don't need to search around for IDs every time you want to IM someone. You can store IDs as part of a contact list:

1. **Starting in the IM service of your choice, press the menu key.**

2. **Touch-press Add a Friend (see Figure 8-7).**

   The Add a Friend screen appears.

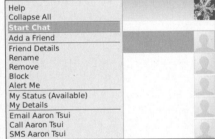

Figure 8-7:
The Google
Talk menu.

3. **Enter your contact's user ID in the Add a Friend screen.**

4. **Touch-press OK.**

   IM is smart enough to figure out whether this contact is a valid user ID. If the ID is valid, the application adds it to your list of contacts. The buddy goes either to the Online or Offline section of your list, depending on whether your buddy is logged in. You're warned if the ID you entered isn't valid.

Doing the chat thing

Suppose you want to start a conversation with one of your contacts (a safe assumption on our part, we think). By sending a message within the IM application, you're initiating a conversation. Here are the details on how to do it:

1. **Log in to the IM application of your choice.**

2. **Touch-press the person you want to contact.**

   A typical online chat screen shows up. The top portion lists old messages sent to and received from this contact. You type your message at the bottom part of the screen.

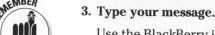

3. **Type your message.**

   Use the BlackBerry in landscape (sideways) mode so it's easier to type.

4. **Touch-press the enter key.**

   Your user ID plus the message you just sent shows up in the topmost (history) section of the chat screen. When you get a message, it's added to the history section so both sides of your conversation stay in view.

Sending your smile

You can quickly add emoticons to your message (without you remembering all the character equivalents in Table 8-2):

1. **While you're typing your message, press the menu key.**

   A menu appears.

2. **Touch-press Show Symbols.**

   All the icons appear.

3. **Touch-press the one you want.**

   The emoticon is added to your message.

Using BlackBerry Messenger

RIM has entered the IM horse race in the form of a spirited filly named — you guessed it — BlackBerry Messenger. This application is based on the PIN-to-PIN messaging technology described earlier in this chapter, which means that it's mucho fast and quite reliable.

However, with BlackBerry Messenger, you can chat with only those buddies who have a BlackBerry and also have PIN-to-PIN messaging enabled.

The application supports IM features common to many of the other applications, such as group chatting and the capability to monitor the availability of other IM buddies.

Running BlackBerry Messenger

Touch-press BlackBerry Messenger from the Home screen. The very first time you run BlackBerry Messenger it asks for two things:

✔ Your display name (see Figure 8-8)

✔ A password (in case you need to restore your contact list in the future)

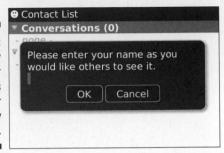

Figure 8-8:
BlackBerry
Messenger
prompts
you to enter
your display
name.

You see a contact list the next time you open the application, as shown on the left in Figure 8-9. (Okay, we know it looks empty here, but we show you how to populate it in a minute.)

Pressing the menu key lets you do these things (see the right side of Figure 8-9):

✔ Customize the groupings

✔ Add a contact

✔ Set your availability

✔ Start a conversation

✔ Change your options

 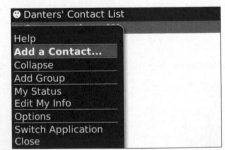

Figure 8-9:
The
BlackBerry
Messenger
contact list
(left) and
menu (right).

Adding a contact

With nobody in your contact list, BlackBerry Messenger is pretty useless. Your first order of business is to add a contact to your list — someone you know who

✔ Has a BlackBerry

✔ Is entered in your Contacts

✔ Has PIN-to-PIN messaging enabled

✔ Has a copy of BlackBerry Messenger installed on her device

If you know someone who fits these criteria, you can add that person to your list by doing the following:

1. **In BlackBerry Messenger, press the menu key.**

2. **Touch-press Add a Contact.**

   All the contacts in your BlackBerry Contacts show up onscreen.

3. **Touch-press the name you want to add to your BlackBerry Messenger contact list.**

   A Message dialog box displays the Permission Request message. BlackBerry sends the request to the potential contact. You can edit the message that's sent.

4. **Type your message.**

5. **Touch-press OK.**

6. **Touch-press OK again.**

   The application sends your request. As long as the person hasn't responded to your request, his name appears as part of the Pending Contacts group, as shown in Figure 8-10. When your contact responds positively to your request, that name goes to the official contact list.

Figure 8-10: To-be-approved contacts are in the Pending Contacts group.

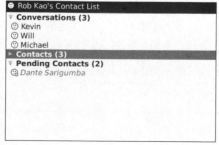

Starting a conversation

You can easily start a conversation with any of your contacts:

1. **In the BlackBerry Messenger main menu, touch-press the name in your contact list.**

   A traditional chat interface opens, with a list of old messages at the top and a text box for typing messages at the bottom.

2. **Type your message.**

3. **Touch-press the enter key.**

   Any messages you send (as well as any responses you get) are appended to the history list at the top.

Starting a group conversation

You can easily invite others to your BlackBerry Messenger conversation:

1. **During a conversation, press the menu key.**

   The BlackBerry Messenger main menu appears. This time an Invite option has been added.

2. **Touch-press Invite.**

   A Select a Contact screen opens.

3. **Touch-press people, one at a time.**

   You can choose any number of people.

4. **Touch-press OK.**

   You're back to the previous conversation screen, but this time the history list text lists the contacts you added to the conversation. The newly selected contact can now join in the conversation.

Taking control of your IM app

If you use IM frequently — and you tend to chat with many contacts all at the same time — your BlackBerry Storm's physical limitations may cramp your IM style. No matter whether you use AIM, Y! Messenger, ICQ, MSN Messenger, or BlackBerry Messenger, it's still slower to type words on the virtual keypad than it is to type on your PC.

Do you just give up on the dream of IMing on the go? Not necessarily. This section shows how you can power up your BlackBerry IM technique.

Less is more

If you can't keep up with all your buddies, your best bet is to limit your exposure. Take a whack at your contact list so that only your true buddies remain as contacts whom you want to IM from your BlackBerry. Trimming your list is easy: Use the Delete option from your BlackBerry Messenger main menu.

Deleting a contact or buddy from an IM application on your BlackBerry also deletes it from the desktop or laptop computer version of the app. That's because the list of contacts is maintained at a central location — an IM server, to be precise — and not on your BlackBerry.

A simple workaround here is to set up two accounts of your favorite IM application — one for your BlackBerry and one for your desktop. By using these accounts separately, you can limit the number of contacts you have on your BlackBerry and still maintain a full-blown list of contacts on your desktop.

Less typing, fewer emoticons

Cut down your typing time. Don't forget the shorthand described previously. It's widely used in IM as well, so refer to Table 8-1 whenever you can so that you can quickly respond. Before you know it, you'll have the abbreviations memorized and use them with ease.

SMS versus connecting via the Web

SMS messages are short messages designed for cellphones. IM is a step up. It provides a better real-time conversation experience across distances. These two technologies evolved in parallel. As more people use IM, it becomes apparent that this technology has a place in handheld devices, where mobility is an advantage. Some of the IM programs developed and used in the BlackBerry in the past use SMS behind the scenes. And because your BlackBerry can connect to the Internet, other programs use the Internet directly. These differences can affect your monthly bill as well as your messaging experience. Read on.

If you don't have unlimited SMS but have an unlimited data plan, be careful for any third-party IM software. Make sure that it's using the Internet instead of SMS. If it's using an SMS, you'll incur charges for every message sent and received. As of this writing, most network providers charge 20 cents for every SMS message. If you're a heavy IM user, 20 cents adds up quickly and will be a nasty surprise on your monthly bill.

Some third-party IM software allows group conversations. This isn't available on the IM software that comes with Storm.

Please check out the Web site associated with this book for updates regarding these (and other) recommendations.

Jive on

Other options exist, such as

✔ **BeejiveIM** at `www.beejive.com/download/blackberry.htm`. This one-time fee program connects directly to the Web instead of using SMS. Works with multiple IM networks, multiple accounts per network: AIM, MSN Messenger, Y! Messenger, GoogleTalk, ICQ, Jabber, and MySpace IM. This is one of the best options.

✔ **Nimbuzz** at `www.nimbuzz.com`. Nimbuzz supports many of the popular IM networks. It even supports calls using the Skype network. And the best thing is it's free and does not use SMS.

✔ **IM+** at `www.shapeservices.com/eng/im/blackberry`. If you don't want to pay annually, consider this service. IM+ only asks for a one-time fee and also supports Yahoo!, MSN, AOL, ICQ, Google Talk, and Jabber networks. The best thing about IM+ is that it sends messages by using the Internet rather than SMS, which is best suited for people who have the unlimited data plan. You have to choose a version: The Regular version connects to BES. BES is used by companies as a way of connecting the BlackBerry platform to the corporate network and e-mail server. The WAP version allows a personal BlackBerry to use the network provider's WAP gateway to connect to the Internet. The Shape Services Web site has a comprehensive FAQ (frequently asked questions) for details about the software.

Chapter 9

Surfing the Internet Wave

*I*t's hard to believe that just over 13 years ago, fewer folks *had* Internet access than didn't. Today, nearly everyone can surf the Web anytime, anywhere, and you can do it with a desktop computer, a laptop computer, or even a tiny mobile device such as a PDA or a SmartPhone. Having said that, it should be no surprise that your Blackberry Storm has a Web browser of its own.

In this chapter, we help you use Blackberry Storm's Browser. We offer shortcuts and throw in timesaving tips, including the coolest ways to make pages load faster and a complete neat-freak's guide to managing your bookmarks.

Your network service provider might also have its own browser for you to use. We compare these *proprietary* (company-specific) browsers with the default BlackBerry Storm's Browser so you can decide which best suits your needs.

Brewing Up a Storm Browser

BlackBerry Storm's Browser comes loaded on your SmartPhone and accesses the Web by a cellphone connection. When you run your Blackberry Storm on BlackBerry Enterprise Server (BES), the application is called *BlackBerry Browser;* otherwise, it's called *Internet Browser*. We just use *Browser* to make things easier.

Blackberry supports multiple browsers and Storm includes two:

✔ One that's connected to your BES server
✔ One that goes directly to your service provider's network

If you're a corporate BlackBerry Storm user, your company administrator might turn off the browser or not install the network service browser. The browser that comes with your network service provider might be called by its brand name.

The following sections get you started using Browser. After you get your feet wet, we promise that you'll be chomping at the bit to find out more!

Getting to the Browser

Browser is one of the main applications of your SmartPhone, with its Globe icon visible on the Home screen, as shown in Figure 9-1. Touch-press this icon to launch Browser. Opening Browser by touch-pressing its icon on the Home screen gives you a list of bookmarks. If you haven't added bookmarks, the opening Browser screen looks like Figure 9-2. You can find out more about adding bookmarks later in this chapter.

Figure 9-1:
You can open Browser from the Home screen.

Figure 9-2:
Browser
with the
default
empty
Bookmarks
screen.

If Browser is your default browser, you can access it from any application that can identify a Web address. For example, from Contacts, you can open Browser by opening the link on the Web Page field. If you get an e-mail containing a Web address, just touch-press that link to open the page. By default, accessing Browser by touch-pressing a Web address within another application opens the Web page associated with that address. (In Figure 9-3, we're opening Browser from the Messages application.)

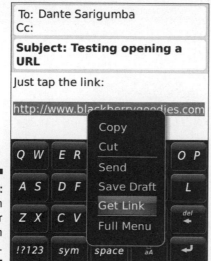

Figure 9-3:
Open
Browser
from
Messages.

Hitting the (air) waves

After you locate Browser, you're ready to surf the Web:

1. **Open Browser.**

2. **Type a Web address.**

   You can see the one we've typed in Figure 9-4.

3. **Touch-press OK.**

   The Web page appears. While the page is loading, progress is indicated at the bottom of the screen.

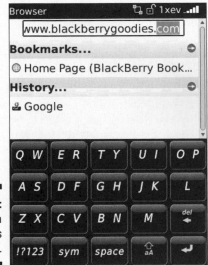

Figure 9-4: Opening a Web page is simple.

When you see a phone number or an e-mail address on a Web page, you can touch-press that information. Touch-pressing initiates a phone call or opens a new e-mail message (depending on which type of link you touched).

Moving around on a Web page

Using Browser to go to a Web page is easy. Note that Web page addresses, also known as *hyperlinks,* are highlighted onscreen. To jump to a particular page, just touch-press the link.

Here are few shortcuts you can use while moving around on a Web page:

✔ To stop loading a page, press the escape key.

✔ After a page is completely onscreen, go back to the previous page by pressing the escape key.

Figure 9-5 points out what you can do with the navigation bar at the bottom of the screen. The images from left to right are shortcuts:

✔ **Star:** Opens the Bookmarks screen.

✔ **www:** Opens the new page, which is the same as touch-pressing Get Link from the menu.

✔ **Page:** Toggles between Page and Column view.

✔ **Arrow pointing left:** Goes back to the previous page.

Figure 9-5:
The naviga-
tion bar.

Open the Bookmarks screen.

Open a new page.

Toggle between Page and Column view.

Go back to previous page.

And don't forget the Browser menu; press the menu key. It has some useful shortcuts, as shown in Figure 9-6.

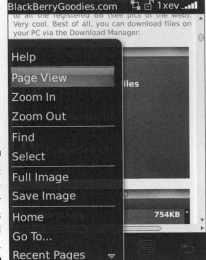 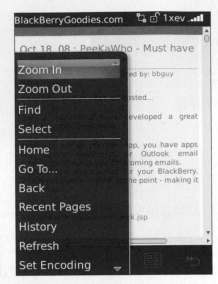

Figure 9-6:
The
Browser
menu has
lots of good
stuff.

The Browser menu offers these options:

- **Page View:** Appears only if you're in Column View. This view allows you to see the page as you'd normally see it on your PC's Internet browser. The compressed version of the Web page takes up the entire screen first. You have the option of zooming in and out available as a menu option.

- **Column View:** This default view normally doesn't appear as a menu option. It shows up only if you're currently in the Page View. The Web page is vertical, meaning a wide Web page wraps down and a scroll bar shows up. Slide the page to see the rest of the contents.

- **Zoom In:** Use this function to make the page more legible. Zooming in makes the Web page not fit the screen, so expect vertical and horizontal scroll bars. Slide the page to pan through the contents. You can zoom in multiple times making the text and images much bigger. After you zoom in, a Zoom Out menu option is available in the menu.

- **Find:** Locates and highlights text on the current page. Like any other basic Find tool, when you choose this option, you type the text you want to find. After the initial search, a Find Next menu appears.

- **Select:** Allows you to highlight a text in the screen for copying.

- **Copy:** This menu item appears only if you've highlighted text. The high-lighted text is copied into memory so you can paste it somewhere else, such as in your MemoPad.

- **Full Image:** This menu item appears only if you highlight an image and only a portion of the image is displayed on the screen.

✔ **Save Image:** Appears when you highlight an image and allows you to save the image in the built-in memory or SD card.

✔ **Home:** The shortcut to your home page. The default home page can vary from carrier to carrier, but to change it:

    1. Bring up the Browser menu.

    2. Touch-press Options⮫Browser Configuration.

    3. Change the Home Page Address field.

✔ **Go To:** Allows you to open a Web page by entering the address and touch-pressing the enter key. As you enter more addresses, the ones you entered before are listed in the History portion of the screen and stored so you don't have to type them again. To find out how to clear that list, see the "Cache operations" section.

✔ **Back <Esc>:** Goes back to the previous page. This menu item only displays if you navigated to more than one Web page.

When you see <Esc>, you can achieve the same function by pressing the escape key.

✔ **Recent Pages:** Browser can track up to 20 pages of Web addresses you've visited, which you can view on the History screen. From there, you can jump to any of those Web pages by highlighting the history page and pressing enter twice.

✔ **History:** Displays a list of the Web pages you visited and allows you to jump back quickly to those pages; it's grouped by date.

✔ **Refresh:** Updates the current page, which is helpful when you're on a page that changes frequently (such as stock quotes or sports scores).

✔ **Set Encoding:** Specifies the encoding in a Web page, which is useful when viewing languages that use something other than English-language characters. Most users don't have to deal with this and might not know what type of encoding a particular language could display.

As a Web page is opening, indicators appear at the bottom of the screen that tell you the progress of your request. The left screen in Figure 9-7 shows Browser requesting a page. The right screen in Figure 9-7 shows you've reached the page and that the page is still loading.

Several icons are in the upper-right corner of both screens in Figure 9-7. We explain them, from right to left:

✔ The **rightmost arrow icons** appear when Browser is processing or receiving data.

✔ The **bars** to the left of the rightmost arrows show the strength of the network signals (the same signal indicator for phone and e-mail).

✔ Your **connection type** also appears; in Figure 9-7, *ev* means the connection is EvDO. (Chapter 1 gives you the scoop on connection types.)

✔ The **lock icon** indicates whether you're at a secure Web page. In this case, it's showing a non-secure page. Whether a page is secure depends on the Web site you're visiting. If you're accessing your bank, you most likely see the secured icon (a closed lock). On the other hand, most pages don't need to be secure, so you see the unsecured icon (an open lock).

The Web address of a secure page starts with `https` rather than `http`.

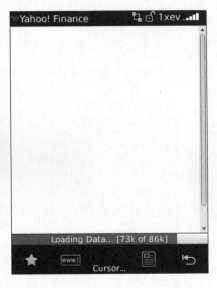

Figure 9-7:
Requesting
a page (left)
and then
loading
(right) it.

If you lose patience waiting for a page to load and want to browse somewhere else, press escape to stop the page from loading.

Saving or sending a Web address

Typing a whole Web address can get tedious. Fortunately, you can return to a page without typing the same address. While you're viewing a Web page, simply use the Browser menu (as shown in Figure 9-8) to save that page's address.

You can save a Web page address in a few ways:

✔ **Page Address:** This option allows you to view the current page's address through a pop-up screen, which gives you two buttons to act on:

• *Copy Address* saves the page's address on your BlackBerry Clipboard and allows you to paste it somewhere else.

• *Send Address* presents another screen so you can choose whether to send the address by e-mail, MMS, PIN, or SMS.

✓ **Send Address:** An alternate way instead of going through Page Address.

✓ **Save Page:** Use this option to save the address of the current page to Messages. A new message with the Browser globe icon to indicate that it's a Web link is added to Messages, as shown in Figure 9-9. Touch-pressing that link launches Browser and opens the page for your viewing pleasure.

Saving a page to your message list has a different purpose than book-marking a page. When you save a page to your message list, you can mark the page as unread, like an e-mail message, to remind yourself to check back later.

Figure 9-8:
Use the Browser menu to save a Web page address.

BlackBerryGoodies.com   1xev

Add Bookmark
Add Web Feed
Bookmarks
Image Address
Page Address
Send Address
Options
Save Page
Show Keyboard
Switch Application
Close

Changing your Home screen background

This trick is neat: Use an image that you've saved on your pictures list as the background (also known as *wallpaper*) on your Home screen. Here's how:

1. **From the Home screen, touch-press the Media icon and touch-press Pictures.**

   The Pictures application opens.

2. **Navigate to the location of the image you want as your background.**

3. **Touch-press the image.**

4. **Press the menu key and touch-press Set as Home Screen Image.**

Figure 9-9:
Save a Web
page link in
Messages.

When you don't have network coverage and try to access a Web page, you're prompted to save your request. When you do, your request is automatically saved in the message list. When you do have coverage later, you can open the same Web page from the message list, with the content loaded already!

Bookmarking Your Favorite Sites

You don't have to memorize your favorite sites' addresses. BlackBerry Browser allows you to keep a list of sites you want to revisit. In other words, make a *bookmark* so you can come back.

Adding a bookmark

Add a new bookmark this way:

1. **Open Browser and go to the Web page you want to bookmark.**

2. **Touch-press Add Bookmark from the Browser menu.**

The menu is always accessible by pressing the menu key.

3. **Type the bookmark name.**

4. **In the Bookmark dialog box, touch-press and navigate to the folder where you want to save the bookmark.**

   The dialog box is shown in Figure 9-10. The default folder is BlackBerry Bookmarks, but you can save the bookmark in folders that you create. To see how to create a bookmark folder, skip to the section, "Adding a subfolder."

5. **Touch-press Add.**

Figure 9-10: Specify the name and the folder in which to store the bookmark.

The next time you want to go to a bookmarked page, do this:

1. **In Browser, touch-press Bookmarks from the Browser menu.**

   You're taken to the Bookmarks screen. From here, you can find all the pages you bookmarked.

2. **Touch-press the bookmark for the page you want to visit.**

Available offline

The Add Bookmark dialog box includes an Available Offline check box, which you might be wondering about. If that check box is selected, you not only save a page as a bookmark, you're also *caching* it so you can see it even when you're out of range (like when you're stuck deep in a mountain cave). Next time you click the bookmark, that page comes up very fast.

We recommend making bookmarks to search engines (such as Google) available offline because the initial search page isn't likely to change from day to day.

Changing a bookmark

Changing a bookmark is a snap:

1. **Touch-press Bookmarks from the Browser menu.**

   The Bookmarks screen opens.

2. **Highlight the name of the bookmark you want to modify.**

3. **Press the menu key and touch-press Edit Bookmark.**

   A screen opens.

4. **Type a new name, a new address, or both.**

5. **Touch-press Accept to save your changes.**

Organizing your bookmarks

Over time, your bookmarks will grow. A tiny screen can make it tough to find a certain site. You can organize your bookmarks by using folders and help work around this problem. For example, you can group related sites in a folder, and each folder can have one or more folders inside it *(subfolders)*. Having subfolders narrows your search and allows you to easily find a site. For example, your sites might fall into these categories:

Reference

NY Times

Yahoo!

Fun

    Flickr

    The Onion

Shopping

    Etsy

    Gaiam

Adding a subfolder

Unfortunately, you can only add subfolders to folders that are already listed on the Bookmark page. Meaning, you can't create your own root folder. Your choices for adding your first subfolder are under WAP Bookmarks or BlackBerry Bookmarks.

Suppose you want to add a Reference subfolder within your BlackBerry Bookmarks folder. Here are the quick and easy steps:

1. **On the Bookmarks screen, touch-press BlackBerry Bookmarks.**

   This is the *parent* of the new subfolder. In this case, the BlackBerry Bookmarks folder will contain the Reference subfolder.

2. **Press the menu key.**

3. **Touch-press Add Subfolder, as shown in Figure 9-11.**

   A dialog box opens.

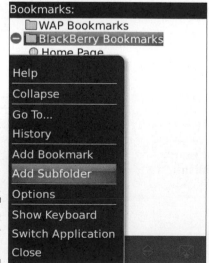

Figure 9-11:
Add a folder here.

4. **Type the name of the folder and then touch-press OK.**

   Reference folder now appears on the Bookmarks screen (as shown in Figure 9-12) with a folder icon.

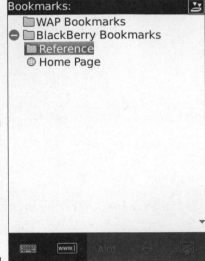

Figure 9-12:
The
Bookmarks
screen
showing the
Reference
folder you
just added.

Renaming a bookmark folder

Renaming a bookmark folder you've created is as easy as editing a bookmark:

1. **Go to the Bookmarks screen.**

2. **Highlight the name of the folder you want to change.**

3. **Press the menu key.**

   A menu appears.

4. **Touch-press Rename Folder.**

5. **Type the name of the folder.**

6. **Touch-press OK to save your changes.**

Moving your bookmarks

If you get lost looking for a bookmark, move that bookmark where it belongs:

1. **Highlight the bookmark you want to move.**

2. **Press the menu key and touch-press Move Bookmark.**

3. **Move the bookmark where you want it.**

   Use the arrow buttons in the bottom navigation bar.

4. **After you find the right location, touch-press the arrows next to the bookmark.**

   Your bookmark is in its new home.

Cleaning up your bookmarks

You may decide you really like a site but then eventually stop visiting it. Or maybe a site disappeared, and every time you click the bookmark you get 404 Not Found. Cleaning up your bookmarks list can help you save time:

1. **Go to the Bookmarks screen.**

2. **Highlight the name of the bookmark you want to delete.**

3. **Press the menu key.**

   A menu appears.

4. **Touch-press Delete Bookmark.**

You can clean up bookmarks wholesale by deleting an entire folder. However, if you delete a folder, you delete *everything* in that folder. Purge with caution.

Exercising Options and Optimizing Techniques

Browser works out of the box. But everyone has their own taste, right? You can look to Browser Options for Browser attributes and features you can customize:

1. **Press the menu key.**

2. **Touch-press Options.**

   The Browser Options screen offers three main categories to choose from, as shown in Figure 9-13:

   - *Browser Configuration:* A place to toggle Browser features.

   - *General Properties:* Settings for general look and feel of the Browser.

   - *Cache Operations:* Gives you ability to clear file caches used by the Browser.

If you feel speed-greedy after adjusting the options, see the upcoming sidebar, "Speeding up browsing."

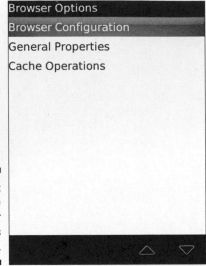

Figure 9-13:
The
Browser
Options
screen.

Configuring Browser

You can define settings from the Browser Configuration screen, which you access from the Browser Options screen. The list of items you can change (as shown in Figure 9-14) are as follows:

✔ **Support JavaScript:** JavaScript is a scripting language used heavily to make dynamic Web pages. A Web page might not behave normally when this option is off.

✔ **Allow JavaScript Popups:** Most ad pages are launched as JavaScript pop-ups. So, having this checked minimizes these ads. But be aware that some important pages are also displayed as JavaScript pop-ups.

✔ **Terminate Slow Running Scripts:** Sometimes there are Web pages with scripts that aren't written well. Keep this selected to keep your Browser from hanging.

✔ **Use Background Images:** A Web page background image can make the Web page look pleasing but if the image is big, it could take time to download it.

✔ **Support Embedded Media:** Embedded Media supported at this point is *scalable vector graphics (SVG)*. Think of it as Flash (which animates your Web pages) for mobile devices, such as the BlackBerry. SVG can be a still image or an animated one.

Figure 9-14:
The
Browser
Configur-
ation
screen.

✓ **Show Images:** Control the display of images depending on the content mode of WML, HTML or both. Think of *WML pages* as Web pages made just for mobile devices, such as the BlackBerry. We recommend leaving this for both.

Turn on and off the display of image placeholders if you opt to not display images.

✓ **Browser Identification:** Specify which browser type your browser emulates. The default is BlackBerry, but Browser can also emulate these instead:

   • Microsoft Internet Explorer

   • Firefox

We don't see much difference in their behavior, so we recommend emulating the default BlackBerry mode.

✓ **Start Page:** Allows you to specify a starting page to load when you open Browser.

✓ **Home Page Address:** Allows you to set your home page. Note that home page is always available from the Browser menu.

General Browser properties

The General Properties screen does the same thing as the Configuration screen: It lets you customize some Browser behaviors. This screen, however, is geared more toward the features of the Browser content. As shown in Figure 9-15, you can do this:

- ✔ Configure features.
- ✔ Turn on features.
- ✔ Turn off features.

Figure 9-15:
The General
Properties
screen.

General Properties

Default Browser: Browser ▼

Default Font Family:
BBAlpha Sans ▼

Default Font Size: 8 ▼

Minimum Font Size: 6 ▼

Minimum Font Style: Plain ▼

Default View: Page ▼

Image Quality: Medium ▼

From this screen, press the Space key to make a change. You can configure the following features by selecting from the choices:

- ✔ **Default Browser:** If you have multiple browsers available, use this to specify which one you want to use when opening a Web link.
- ✔ **Default Font Family:** When a Web page doesn't specify the text font, Browser will use the one you selected here.
- ✔ **Default Font Size:** When a Web page doesn't specify the text font size, Browser will use the one you selected here. The smaller the size, the more text fits on the screen.
- ✔ **Minimum Font Size:** A Web page may specify a font size too small to be legible. Specifying a legible font size will override the Web page.

✔ **Minimum Font Style:** When Browser is using the minimum font size, you can choose what font to use. Some fonts are more legible even in small size than others. If you're not sure which one to use, leave the default untouched.

✔ **Default View:** You can toggle the default view:

- *Column* wraps all Web page elements vertically, so you just scroll up and down by panning the page.

- *Desktop* displays the page like you normally see in your PC's Internet browser. Pan the page to scroll left, right, up, and down.

✔ **Image Quality:** The higher the quality, the slower the page loads. The default quality is medium. You have three options: low, medium, or high.

✔ **Repeat Animations:** Set the number of times an animation repeats. The default is 100, but you can change this setting:

- Never

- Once

- 10 Times

- 100 Times

- As Many as the Image Specifies

✔ **Full Screen View:** Makes the page displayed in compressed format so that you can see the whole page.

✔ **Enable JavaScript Location Support:** Web pages that have scripts that take advantage of your BlackBerry's location through GPS will work if you have this selected.

✔ **Prompting Before:** You can have BlackBerry Browser give you a second chance before you do the following things:

- *Closing Browser on Escape:* You're notified right before you exit BlackBerry Browser.

- *Closing Modified Pages:* You're notified right before you exit a modified Web page (for example, some type of online form you fill out).

- *Running WML Scripts: WML* is a script to tell a wireless device how to display a page. It was popular years back when resolutions of device screens were low, but very few Web sites are using it now. We recommend leaving this field deselected, as this type of scripting is old and benign.

Cache operations

At any given time, your Blackberry uses a few cache mechanisms. A *cache* (pronounced *cash*) temporarily stores information used by Browser so the next time the info is needed, Browser doesn't have to go back to the source Web site. The cache can speed up displays when you want to see the Web page again and is useful when you're suddenly out of network coverage. When you visit a site that uses *cookies* (think of a cookie as a piece of text that a Web site created and placed in your BlackBerry's memory to remember something about you), Browser caches that cookie.

Browser also caches pages and content so you can see them while you're *offline* (not connected to the Internet). Viewing pages offline is handy when you're out of range.

Some Web sites *push* (send information) Web pages to BlackBerry SmartPhones. An icon appears on the Home screen allowing you to quickly view the page. After the Web page is delivered in your BlackBerry, it becomes available even if you go out of coverage. If you subscribed to this service, your device stores Web pages in the cache. Also, the addresses of the pages that you visited (or the 20 in your history list) comprise a cache.

The Cache Operations screen, shown in Figure 9-16, allows you to manually clean your cache. You can find Cash Operations by following these steps:

1. **From the Browser screen, press the menu key.**

2. **Touch-press Options.**

3. **Touch-press Cache Operation.**

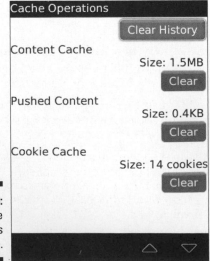

Figure 9-16:
The Cache
Operations
screen.

Speeding up browsing

Many things can affect how quickly Web pages appear on a wireless device. If browsing the Web is extremely slow, you can make your pages load faster in exchange for not using a few features:

✔ **Don't display images.** You can see a big performance improvement by turning off images. From the Browser menu, touch-press Options➪Browser Configuration, and change the value to No on Show Images.

✔ **Make sure your BlackBerry isn't low on or out of memory.** When your BlackBerry's memory is very low, its performance degrades. The BlackBerry low-memory manager calls each application every now and then, telling each one to free up resources.

Hint: Don't leave many e-mail messages unread. When the low-memory manager kicks in, your BlackBerry Storm will try to delete old e-mails and SMS messages, but it can't delete unread ones.

✔ **Turn off other features.** If you're mostly interested in content, consider turning off features, such as Use Background Images, Support JavaScript, and Allow JavaScript Popups. To turn off other browser features, navigate to Browser Options➪General Properties.

Warning: Don't turn off features while performing an important task, such as online banking. If you do, you might not be able to perform some of the actions on the page. For example, the Submit button might not work.

The Cache Operations screen shows the size of each type of cache. You also see the Clear button if the cache has content. Touch-press Clear to delete the specified cache type. Touch-press Clear History to erase the history list of the Web sites you visited.

Cache comes in four types:

✔ **Content Cache:** Any offline content. You might want to clear this whenever you're running out of space on your BlackBerry. Or maybe you're tired of viewing old content or sick of pressing the Refresh option.

✔ **Pushed Content:** Any content that was pushed to your Blackberry from Push Services subscriptions. You might want to clear this to free memory on your Blackberry.

✔ **Cookie Cache:** Any cookies stored on your BlackBerry. Nowadays, almost all Web sites use cookies, and the information inside it can be used to gather information about you and your Web-browsing habits. You might want to clear out this for security's sake. Sometimes you don't want a Web site to remember you.

✔ **History:** Sites you've visited by using the Go To function. You might want to clear this for the sake of security if you don't want other people knowing which Web sites you're visiting on your BlackBerry.

Installing and Uninstalling Applications from the Web

You can download and install applications on your BlackBerry by using Browser. That is, if the application has a link that lets you download and install the files. The downloading and installing parts are easy:

1. **Click the link from Browser.**

   It displays a simple prompt that looks like the screen shown in Figure 9-17.

2. **Click the Download button.**

   The download starts.

Figure 9-17: A typical page letting you download an application on your BlackBerry Storm.

As long as you stay within network coverage during the download, your BlackBerry can finish the download *and* install the application for you. If it finishes without any problems, you see a screen similar to Figure 9-18.

Figure 9-18:
The download and installation was completed.

As with a desktop computer, the download might or might not work.

Sometimes the application requires that you install libraries, and sometimes the application works only on a certain version of the BlackBerry OS. These issues can be prevented, depending on the site where the link is. With most reputable sources, these issues are considered — and successful downloading and installation are a snap.

Installing applications from nonreputable sources can make your BlackBerry unstable. Before you download an application from the Web, read reviews about that particular application. Most of the time, other people who tried the software provide reviews or feedback. Don't be the first to write the bad review!

You BES administrator can disable the feature in your BlackBerry to download and install an application. This is mostly the case for a company-issued device. If you have problems downloading and installing an application, check your company policy or contact the BlackBerry support person in your company.

If you download an application that turns out to be a dud, you need to uninstall it. See Chapter 17 for more on uninstalling an application from your BlackBerry.

Browser Behavior in Business

Getting a BlackBerry from your employer has two sides:

- ✔ On the good side, your company foots the bill.
- ✔ On the bad side, your company foots the bill.

Because your company pays, the company dictates what you can and can't do with your BlackBerry device. This is especially true with respect to browsing the Web.

Two scenarios come into play when it comes to your browser:

- ✔ Your browser might be running under your company's *BlackBerry Enterprise Server (BES)*. With this setup, your BlackBerry Browser is connecting to the Internet by using your company's Internet connection. It's like using your desktop machine at work.
- ✔ Your browser is connected through a network service provider. Most of the time, this kind of browser is called by the company's name.

In most cases, your device fits in one scenario, which is the case where your browser is connected through your company's BES server. Some lucky folks might have both. Whatever scenario you're in, the following sections describe the major differences between the two.

Using Browser on your company's BES

When your BlackBerry Storm comes from your company, Browser is connected through your company's BES server. With this setup, the browser is actually named *BlackBerry Browser*. BES is in your company's local network referred to as *intranet,* as opposed to being visible publicly like the Internet. This setup allows the company to better manage the privileges and the functions you can use on your device.

For the BlackBerry Browser, this setup lets the company use the existing Internet, including the company's *firewall* (which helps with online safety). Because you're within the company's network, the boundaries set up on your account apply to your BlackBerry as well. For example, when browsing the Web, your BlackBerry won't display any Web sites that are blocked by your company's server.

The good thing, though, is that you can browse by using the company's intranet. Meaning, all the Web pages you have access to inside your company through your company's PC are also available in your BlackBerry.

Know your company's Web-browsing policy. Most companies log the sites you view and might even have software to monitor usage. Also, your company might not allow downloading from the Web.

Using your network provider's browser

Any new device coming from a network service provider can come with its own branded Web browser. The network browser is the same as the BlackBerry Browser, but the behavior might differ:

- **The name is different.**

- **The default home page usually points to the provider's Web site.** This isn't necessarily a bad thing. Most of the time, the network provider's Web site is full of links that you might not find on BlackBerry Browser.

- **You can browse more sites.** You're not limited by your company's policy.

Most of the time, surfing the Web is much faster if your browser is through BES. This isn't true all the time, however, because the network bandwidth or data pipe used by your BES affects how much data can travel on those pipes, the size of those pipes, and the speed that Browser loads the page.

Setting the default browser

If you have two Web browsers on your device, you can set the *default* browser. This comes into play when you view a Web address by using a link outside Browser application. For example, when you view an e-mail with a Web link, touch-pressing that link will launch the default browser.

To set up the default browser, do this:

1. **Go to the Home screen.**

2. **Touch-press Settings⇨Options⇨Advanced Options⇨Browser.**

3. **Touch-press the selections in the Default browser configuration.**

    Figure 9-19 shows the Browser Settings screen with the default browser selected.

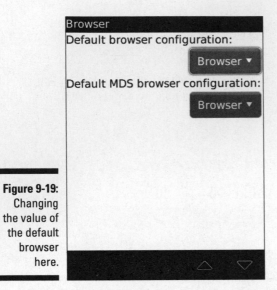

Figure 9-19:
Changing
the value of
the default
browser
here.

Chapter 10

Calling Your Favorite Person

The BlackBerry phone operates no differently than any other phone you've used. Why bother with this chapter? Your BlackBerry phone can do things your run-of-the-mill cellphone can't. For example, when was the last time your phone was connected to your to-do list? Have you ever received an e-mail and placed a call directly from that e-mail? We didn't think so. But with your BlackBerry, you can do all these things and more.

Using the BlackBerry Phone Application

The folks at RIM have created an intuitive user interface to all the essential Phone features, including making and receiving calls.

Making a call

To make a call, follow these steps:

1. **Press the green send key.**

2. **Touch-press the phone number of the person you want to call.**

3. **Press the green send key again to call.**

Calling from Contacts

Because you can't possibly remember all your friends' and colleagues' phone numbers, calling from Contacts is convenient and useful. To call from Contacts, follow these steps:

1. **Press the green send key.**

   The Phone application opens.

2. **Press the menu key.**

   The Phone menu appears.

3. **Touch-press Call from Contacts.**

   Contacts opens. From here, you can search as usual for the contact you'd like to call.

4. **From Contacts, touch-press your call recipient.**

5. **Press the green send key.**

   This makes the call.

Using a calling card or dialing an extension

Have you ever dialed a long-distance number using a calling card? First you call the calling-card access number, then you enter the code, then you dial the long-distance number. Major pain in the behind. Although not as bad, dialing someone's extension isn't fun either.

In Contacts, under the Contact Phone Number field, you add x with the extension number. The next time you call that contact, a screen asks if you want the extension dialed for you; see Figure 10-1. You can do the same with a calling-card access number, but add the access number and x in front of the phone number.

For example, if you're in the U.S. and using a calling card for a UK number, the phone number field in Contacts would look like this: 800-555-1314x011-44-775-555-1212. The phone number is 011-44-775-555-1212; the calling card access number is 800-555-1314.

Getting a call

Receiving a call on your BlackBerry is even easier than making a call. You can receive calls in a couple of ways:

✔ **Use your automated answering feature.** Automated answering is triggered whenever you take your BlackBerry out of your holster; in other words, just taking out the BlackBerry forces it to automatically pick up any call, so you can start talking right away. The disadvantage of this is that you don't have time to see who is calling you (on your Caller ID).

✔ **Answer manually.** When you get a call, your screen will look something like Figure 10-2. Just touch-press Answer to pick up the phone.

Figure 10-1:
Using a calling card to call international with ease.

Figure 10-2:
There's an incoming call for you!

To disable auto answering, make sure Auto Answer Call option is set to Never. You can get to Auto Answer Call option by pressing the menu key from the Phone application and then touch-press Option from the Phone menu.

What's the advantage of disabling auto answering? Manual answering allows you to answer or ignore when you receive a call, as shown in Figure 10-3. This way, you can see on your Caller ID who's calling; you can pick up or ignore.

Figure 10-3:
What the BlackBerry Storm screen looks like while on a call.

Muting your call

Muting lets you hear but not be heard. This option is useful when you're on a conference call. (See the upcoming section, "Arranging Conference Calls.") Maybe you're on the bus or have kids in the background.

To mute or unmute your call, toggle the Mute icon.

Putting someone on hold

If you put someone on hold, neither you nor your caller can hear each another. To put a conversation on hold

1. **While in a conversation, press the menu key.**

   The Phone menu appears yet again.

2. **Touch-press Hold.**

   Your call is now on hold.

To un-hold your call

1. **While a call is on hold, press the menu key.**

   A new menu appears.

2. **Touch-press Resume.**

   You can continue your conversation again.

Turning down the volume

You can adjust the call volume, a simple yet important action on your BlackBerry phone, by pressing the volume up or down key on the side of your BlackBerry Storm during a call.

Customizing Your Phone

For your BlackBerry phone to work the way you like, you have to first set it up the way you want it. This section offers some settings that can make you the master of your BlackBerry phone.

Setting up your voice mail number

This section shows you how to set up your voice mail access number. Unfortunately, the instructions for setting up your voice mailbox vary, depending on your service provider. But usually you can access the voice mail by pressing the menu key in the Phone application and touch-pressing the Call Voice Mail option.

Most service providers are more than happy to walk you through the steps to get your mailbox set up in a jiffy.

To set up your voice mail access number:

1. **Press the green send key.**

   The Phone application opens.

2. **Press the menu key.**

3. **Select the options item.**

   A list of phone options appears.

4. **Select Voice Mail.**

   This opens the Voice Mail Configuration screen.

5. **In the Access the Number field, type your voice mail access number.**

   If this field is empty and you don't know this number, contact your service provider and ask for your voice mail access number. Typically, it's your mobile number.

6. **Press the menu key.**

7. **Select Save.**

Using call forwarding

The BlackBerry has two types of call forwarding:

- **Forward All Calls:** Any calls to your BlackBerry are forwarded to the number you designate. Another name for this feature is *unconditional forwarding.*

- **Forward Unanswered Calls:** Calls that meet different types of conditions are forwarded to different numbers as follows:

  - *If Busy:* You don't have call waiting turned on, and you're on the phone.

  - *If No Answer:* You don't hear your phone ring or can't pick up your phone. (Perhaps you're in a meeting.)

  - *If Unreachable:* You're out of network coverage and can't get a signal.

Out of the box, your BlackBerry forwards any unanswered calls, regardless of conditions, to your voice mail number by default. However, you can add new numbers to forward a call to.

You need to be within network coverage before you can change your call forwarding option. After you're within network coverage, you can change your call forwarding settings by doing the following:

1. **Press the green send key.**

   The Phone application opens.

2. **Press the menu key.**

3. **Touch-press Options menu item.**

   A list of phone options appears.

4. **Touch-press Call Forwarding.**

   Your BlackBerry attempts to connect to the server. If successful, you see the Call Forwarding screen.

   If you don't see the Call Forwarding screen, wait until you have network coverage and try again.

5. **Press the menu key and touch-press Edit Numbers.**

   A list of numbers appears. If this is the first time you're setting call forwarding, mostly likely your voice mail number is the only one on the list.

6. **To add a new forwarding number, press the menu key and touch-press New Number.**

   A pop-up menu prompts you to type the number.

7. **Type the number.**

   The new number you entered now appears on the call forward list. You can add this new number to any call forwarding types or conditions.

8. **Press the escape key.**

   You return to the Call Forwarding screen.

9. **Touch-press If Unreachable field.**

   A drop-down menu lists numbers from the call forward list, including the one you just added.

10. **Touch-press the number you want to forward to and then touch-press to confirm.**

    The selected number appears in the If Unreachable field. You can see this on the Call Forwarding screen.

11. **Press the menu key and touch-press Save.**

    Your changes are confirmed.

Arranging Conference Calls

To have two (or more) people on the phone with you — the infamous *conference call* — do the following:

1. **Use the Phone application to call the first person.**

2. **While the first participant is on the phone with you, touch-press the Conference button on screen, as shown in Figure 10-3.**

   This automatically places the first call on hold and brings up a New Call screen.

3. **Type the phone number for the second person.**

   You can dial the number a number of ways:

   - Using the onscreen number pad.
   - Selecting a frequently dialed number from your call log.

   To place a call from your Contacts, press the menu key from the New Call screen and select Call from Contact. Your BlackBerry prompts you to select a contact.

4. **Press the green send key.**

   The call to the second meeting participant is just like any other phone call (except the first participant is still on hold on the other line).

5. **While the second person is on the phone with you, press the menu key and touch-press Join Conference, as shown in Figure 10-4.**

   This connects the first and second participants. Now you can discuss with both participants at the same time.

Figure 10-4: Join two people in a conference call.

Having two people on the phone with you is also known as *three-way calling*. If you want to chat with four people — or even ten people — at the same time, you certainly can. Simply repeat Steps 2–5 until all the participants are on the phone.

Talking privately to a conference participant

During a conference call, you might want to talk to one person privately. This is called *splitting* your conference call. Here's how you do it:

1. **While on a conference call, press the menu key.**

2. **Touch-press Split Call.**

   A pop-up screen lists all the conference call participants

3. **Touch-press the person you want to speak with privately.**

   This puts all other participants on hold and connects you to the participant you selected. On the display screen, you can see who you're connected to; this confirms that you chose the right person to chat with privately.

4. **To talk to all participants again, press the menu key and touch-press Join Conference.**

Alternating between phone conversations

Whether you're in a private conversation during a conference call or you're talking to someone while you have someone else on hold, you can switch between the two conversations by *swapping* them. Follow these steps:

1. **While talking to someone, press the menu key and touch-press Hold.**

   That person is put on hold.

2. **Press the menu key and touch-press Swap.**

   You switch from the person with whom you're currently talking to the person who was on hold.

3. **Repeat Step 2 to go back to the original conversation.**

Dropping that meeting hugger

If you've been on conference calls, you know those chatty "meeting huggers" who have to say something about everything. Don't you wish you could drop them from the call? With your BlackBerry, you can (as long as you initiated the call):

1. **While on a conference call, press the menu key.**

2. **Touch-press Drop Call.**

   A pop-up screen lists all conference-call participants.

3. **Touch-press the person you want to drop.**

   That person is disconnected.

4. **Continue the conversation with the other people.**

Communicating Hands Free

More and more places prohibit the use of mobile phones without a hands-free headset. Luckily for you, BlackBerry offers hands-free options.

Using the speaker phone

The Speaker Phone function is useful under certain situations, such as when you're in a room full of people who want to join in the conversation. Or you might be all by your lonesome in your office but are stuck rooting through your files — hard to do with a BlackBerry scrunched up against your ear. (We call such moments *multitasking* — a concept so important we devote an entire upcoming section to it.)

To switch to the speaker phone while you're on a phone call, press the Speaker button on screen; see Figure 10-3.

Pairing your BlackBerry with a Bluetooth headset

Your Storm comes with a wired hands-free headset, so you can start using yours by plugging it into the headset jack on the left side of the Storm. You adjust the headset's volume by pressing up or down on the volume keys.

Using the wired hands-free headset can help, but the wired headset can get in the way if you're multitasking on your BlackBerry. The whole Bluetooth wireless thing comes in here. You can buy a Bluetooth headset to go with your Bluetooth-enabled BlackBerry.

After you purchase a Bluetooth headset, you can pair it with your BlackBerry Storm. Think of *pairing* a Bluetooth headset with your Storm as registering the headset with your Storm so that it recognizes the headset.

First things first: You need to prep your headset for pairing. Now, each headset manufacturer has a different take on this, so consult your headset documentation for details.

With that out of the way, continue with the pairing as follows:

1. **From the Home screen, press the menu key.**

2. **Touch-press the Wireless Connections.**

   A pop-up screen appears.

3. **Touch-press the Enable check box next to Bluetooth and then touch-press Set Up Bluetooth.**

   If this is the first time you're using Bluetooth, you're asked to set a name for your device so others can see your Storm when trying to connect to you via Bluetooth.

   If this isn't the first time, you will see a Add Device pop-up screen with the following buttons:

   - *Search:* If you want to reach out to other device

   - *Listen:* If you want other device to find you.

   - *Cancel:* If you want to cancel this operation.

4. **Touch-press Search.**

   You see the Searching for Devices progress bar, um, progressing. When your BlackBerry discovers the headset, a Select Device dialog box appears with the name of the headset.

5. **Touch-press the Bluetooth headset.**

   A dialog box prompts you for a passkey code to the headset.

6. **Type the passkey and touch-press Okay.**

   Normally the Bluetooth passkey is 0000 but refer to your headset documentation.

   After you successfully enter the passkey, your headset is listed in the Bluetooth setting.

7. **Press the menu key.**

   The Bluetooth menu appears.

8. **Touch-press Connect.**

   Your BlackBerry attempts to connect to the Bluetooth headset.

Using your voice to dial

With your headset and the Voice Dialing application, you can truly be hands free. You may be wondering how to activate the Voice Dialing application without touching your BlackBerry. Good question. The majority of hands-free headsets (Bluetooth or not) come with a multipurpose button.

Usually, a multipurpose button on a hands-free headset can mute, end, and initiate a call. Refer to your hands-free headset manual for more info.

1. **Activate your headset.**

2. **Press its multipurpose button.**

   The Voice Dialing application is activated and a voice states, "Say a command."

3. **Say "Call *name of person* or *number*."**

The Voice Dialing application is good at recognizing the name of the person and the numbers you dictate. However, we strongly suggest that you try the voice dialing feature before you need it.

Taking Notes While on the Phone

You're not stuck just talking to someone on the phone. When you're on your BlackBerry, you can use it for other tasks at the same time. Why not

- ✓ Take meeting notes while you're in a conference call?
- ✓ Look up a phone number in the BlackBerry Contacts that your caller is asking you for?
- ✓ Make a to-do list while you're planning the party?
- ✓ Compose an e-mail thanking the caller for his time?

It makes sense to multitask while you're using a hands-free headset or a speaker phone. Otherwise, your face would be stuck to your BlackBerry.

After you don your hands-free headset or turn on a speaker phone, you can start multitasking:

1. **While in a conversation, from the Phone application, press the icon that looks like a house.**

   This gets you to the Home screen.

2. **Start multitasking.**

   While on the phone and multitasking, you can access the Phone menu from other applications. For example, you can end a call or put a call on hold from your to-do list.

Do this to take notes of your call:

1. **During a phone conversation, press the menu key.**

   Or you can press the notepad icon in Figure 10-3; if you do, then go to Step 3.

2. **Touch-press Notes.**

   The Notes screen appears.

3. **Type notes for the conversation, as shown in Figure 10-5.**

   When the call ends, the notes are automatically saved for you.

Figure 10-5:
Take notes
while on a
phone call.

Accessing phone notes

From the Call History list, you can access notes you've made during a call. In addition, you can also edit and add new notes.

1. **Press the green send key.**

   The Phone application opens. If you have calls from before, you see a screen like Figure 10-6.

2. **Touch-press a call log to highlight it.**

3. **Press the menu key and touch-press View History.**

   The Call History screen (see Figure 10-7) opens for the highlighted call.

4. **Press the menu key.**

5. **Choose one of the following:**

   - *Add Notes:* If the call has no notes.
   - *Edit Notes:* If the call already has notes.

Figure 10-6: A screen showing call logs.

```
Call History
18002123232
18002123232
Type: Received Call
Duration: 5:48
Date: 28/10/2008 02:19
Remember this...




Total Calls: 1
              △      ▽
```

Figure 10-7:
Call History, where you can see conversation notes.

Forwarding phone notes

You can forward your phone notes just like an e-mail:

1. **While in the Call History screen (see Figure 10-7), press the menu key.**

2. **Touch-press Forward.**

    A new e-mail opens with the body of the e-mail filled with call details and notes. You can forward call notes via e-mail (no SMS or PIN messages). You can send the e-mail as you would any other e-mail. See Chapter 8 for more information on e-mails.

Chapter 11

Taking Great Pictures with Your Storm

*O*h shoot, you forgot your camera. Don't worry! Your Storm's there when you need to capture the unbelievable: Grandma's doing a handstand, your Grandpa is doing a cartwheel, or your roommate is doing her laundry.

Before you try taking pictures with it, read this chapter so you know what to expect and how to get the best shot. We also walk you through the easy steps in capturing that funny pose. We also tell you how to store those shots and share them with your buddies.

Saying "Cheese"

Before you ask someone to pose, examine your BlackBerry Storm (shown in Figure 11-1) first:

▶ **Is the camera on?** You see the bottom key on the right side of your BlackBerry Storm? Press it to bring up the Camera application. Alternatively, you can touch-press the Camera icon from the Home screen.

▶ **Is your finger blocking the lens?** The lens is on the back side of your device.

▶ **Do you see the image in the screen?** Pressing the camera key again takes the picture. You should hear a funky sound. Neat and easy, isn't it?

Itching to take more pictures? Hold those snapping fingers of yours. If you take a few moments first to familiarize yourself with the camera's features, the effort could go a long way.

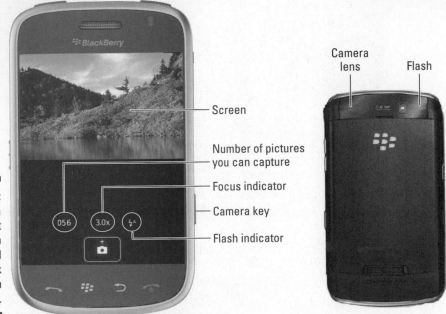

Figure 11-1:
The camera
items, front
screen
(left), and
the back
of Storm
(right).

Reading the screen indicators

When you open the Camera, the first thing you see is the screen in Figure 11-2. The top portion of this screen shows the image you're about to capture. The bottom part contains icons (starting from the left) that indicate the following:

- ✔ Number of pictures you can capture
- ✔ Focus
- ✔ Flash

Choosing the picture quality

BlackBerry Storm can capture up to 3.2 megapixels (mp) of resolution. Saving at this resolution requires a big space. You can save at a lower quality and save some space on your BlackBerry:

- ✔ Normal
- ✔ Fine
- ✔ SuperFine

Figure 11-2:
The Camera
screen
ready
to take
pictures.

056   3.0x   ⚡ᴬ

The default camera setting is Normal, which is the lowest quality but lets you save the most pictures. The trade-off is that a Normal picture won't be as smooth or fine. Choose a setting based on how you plan to use the picture. If you're shooting a breathtaking landscape and want to capture every possible detail for printing later, use the SuperFine setting. If you're just taking pictures of your friends' faces so you can attach them as Caller ID, Normal is appropriate.

Changing picture quality is a snap:

1. **Press the bottom key on the right side of your Storm.**

   The Camera application opens.

2. **Press the menu key.**

3. **Touch-press Options.**

   The Options screen appears, as shown in Figure 11-3.

4. **Touch-press Picture Quality.**

5. **Touch-press the picture quality you want from the available selections.**

   Picture Quality values to choose from are Normal, Fine, and SuperFine.

6. **Press the menu key.**

7. **Touch-press Save.**

   The picture quality you've chosen is now active.

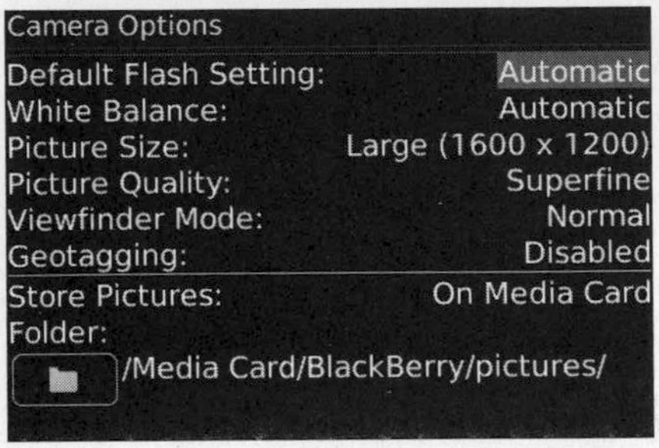

Figure 11-3:
The camera
Options
screen.

```
Camera Options
Default Flash Setting:              Automatic
White Balance:                      Automatic
Picture Size:           Large (1600 x 1200)
Picture Quality:                     Superfine
Viewfinder Mode:                       Normal
Geotagging:                           Disabled
Store Pictures:             On Media Card
Folder:
    ▶  /Media Card/BlackBerry/pictures/
```

Zooming and focusing

You need to be steady to get a good focus while taking the shots. Although it's convenient to use one hand while taking pictures, most of the time you'll get a blurry image if you try that.

When taking pictures, hold your BlackBerry with both hands, one holding the device steady and the other clicking the button.

Holding the camera with both hands is even more important if you're zooming in. Yes, your camera is capable of up to 2x digital zoom. Here's what you need to do for focusing and zooming:

- ✔ **To focus:** Press the camera key halfway.
- ✔ **To zoom in:** Slide finger up.
- ✔ **To zoom out:** Slide finger down.

While zooming, the value in the indicator changes from 1x, 2x, up to 3x and vice versa, depending on the direction you scroll.

Setting the flash

The rightmost indicator on the Camera screen is the flash. The default is Automatic, which shows an arrow with the letter *A*. Automatic means it goes off if it doesn't detect enough light. Where it's dark, the flash fires; otherwise, it doesn't.

You can turn the flash on or off. When set to off, the arrow image is slashed through, just like you see on the Don't Walk traffic signal. You can toggle the settings in Camera's Options screen. (Press the menu key and touch-press Options to get to the Options screen.)

Setting the white balance

In photography, filters are used to compensate for the dominant light. For instance, a fluorescent versus an incandescent light could affect how warm the picture looks. Instead of using filters, most digital cameras have a feature to correct or compensate for many types of light settings. This feature is *White Balance.* And yes, your Storm, of course, has one. You can choose from Sunny, Cloudy, Night, Incandescent, Fluorescent, or Automatic. *Automatic* means your camera sets what it thinks are the best settings to apply.

You can change the white balance through the camera's Options screen.

The camera's Options screen is accessible by pressing the menu key and touch-pressing Options from the menu that follows.

Setting the picture size

Aside from picture quality, you can also adjust the actual size of the photo:

- ✔ **Large:** 1600 x 1200
- ✔ **Medium:** 1024 x 768
- ✔ **Small:** 640 x 480

Again, camera settings are accessible through the camera's Options screen by pressing the menu key and touch-pressing Options from the menu that shows.

Geotagging

With your Storm having a GPS capability, your location based on longitude and latitude can be determined easily. This information can be added to your media files including the pictures taken from your camera. Adding geographic information is referred to as *Geotagging.* On your Storm, it adds longitude and latitude information. Now, you don't have to wonder where you took that crazy pose.

Geotagging by default is disabled in your Storm. You can simply enable it from the camera Options screen. (Press the menu key and touch-press Options to get to the Options screen.)

TIP

If you have longitude and latitude information from one of your photos, you can use one of the free sites on the Web to locate that information in the map. One such site is www.travelgis.com/geocode/Default.aspx.

Working with Pictures

You've taken a bunch of pictures and you want to see them. And maybe delete the unflattering ones. Or perhaps organize them. No problem.

Viewing pictures

If you take a picture, you want to see it, right? *Viewing* a picture is a common function with your camera. You can see the image you just captured right then and there, as shown in Figure 11-4.

TIP

If you're browsing through your picture folders, you can view a picture by simply touch-pressing the picture file.

Figure 11-4:
The Camera
screen after
taking a
picture.

IMG 00003-20081026-2251

Creating a slide show

Want to see your pictures in a slide show?

1. **While in Camera screen, press the menu key and touch-press View Pictures from the menu that appears.**

2. **Press the menu key.**

3. **Touch-press Slide Show.**

   Voilà! Your BlackBerry Storm displays your pictures one at a time at a regular time interval. The default interval between each picture is two seconds; if you're not happy with this interval, change it in the Options screen. (Press the menu key and touch-press Options to get to the Options screen.)

Trashing

If you don't like the image you captured, you can delete it.

1. **Highlight the picture you want trashed.**

2. **Touch-press the Delete (X) icon.**

   A confirmation screen comes up.

3. **Touch-press Delete.**

   You can do the same thing right after taking the picture; just touch-press the trash can icon when viewing the photo. Refer to Figure 11-4.

Listing filenames versus thumbnails

When you open a folder packed with pictures, your BlackBerry automatically lists *thumbnails,* which are small previews of your pictures.

A preview is nice, but what if you're looking for a picture and know the file name? Wouldn't it be nice to see a list of names instead of thumbnails?

1. **Go to a picture folder.**

2. **Press the menu key.**

3. **Touch-press View List.**

That's exactly what you get: a list of all the pictures in the folder. What's neat is that the option also displays the file size. The file size can give you a clue of what settings you used to take the picture. For example, a photo taken from a SuperFine quality produces a much bigger file size compared to normal.

Checking picture properties

Curious about the amount of memory your picture is using? Want to know the time you took the photo?

1. **Highlight the picture from a list.**

    While you're in Camera screen, you can view the list of your pictures by pressing the menu key and touch-pressing View Pictures.

2. **Press the menu key.**

3. **Touch-press Properties.**

    You see a screen similar to Figure 11-5, which displays the picture's location, size, and last modification.

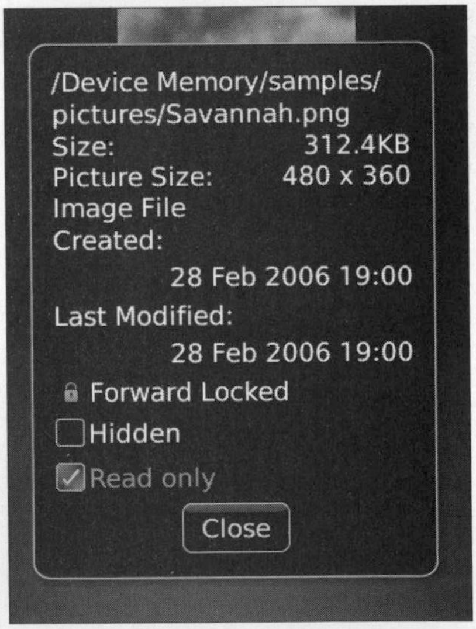

Figure 11-5:
Your picture
properties.

Organizing your pictures

Organization is all about time and the best use of it. After all, you want to enjoy looking at your pictures — not looking for them. You want to organize your pictures; you can change how they're stored and how they're named. Plus, you can create folders. With those capabilities, you should be on your way to organization nirvana.

Renaming a picture file

BlackBerry saves a file when you capture a picture. However, the file name is generic, something like IMG*xxxx,* where the *x* is a number.

Make it a habit to rename the file as soon as you've finished capturing the picture. It is easier to recognize *Dean blows birthday candles* than *IMG00003-20081013-0029.*

Renaming is a snap. Here's how:

1. **Display the picture onscreen or highlight it in the list.**

2. **Press the menu key.**

3. **Touch-press Rename.**

    A Rename screen appears.

4. **Type the name you want for this picture.**

5. **Touch-press Save.**

    Your picture is renamed.

Creating a new folder

Being the organized person you are, you must be wondering about folders. Don't fret; it's simple to create one:

1. **In the Camera screen, press the menu key.**

2. **Touch-press View Pictures.**

    The screen displays the list of pictures in the current folder and an Up icon for you to navigate to the folder above this.

3. **Touch-press the Up icon.**

4. **Navigate to the main folder where you want your new folder to be created.**

   You should be *within* the folder where you want your new folder to be created. If not, repeat this step to navigate to that folder.

5. **Press the menu key.**

6. **Touch-press New Folder.**

7. **Enter the name of the folder.**

8. **Touch-press OK.**

   Your folder is created.

Moving pictures

There are many reasons for moving pictures between folders. The most obvious reason is to organize your pictures. Want to try it? Follow these steps:

1. **In the Camera screen, press the menu key.**

2. **Touch-press View Pictures.**

   The screen lists pictures in the current folder. If the picture you want to move isn't in this folder, touch-press the Up icon to navigate up to other folders.

3. **Highlight the picture you want to move.**

4. **Press the menu key.**

5. **Touch-press Move.**

   The screen allows you to go to the folder where you want to move this picture.

6. **Touch-press the Up icon.**

7. **Navigate to the folder where you want to move this picture.**

8. **Press the menu key.**

9. **Touch-press Move Here.**

   Your picture is moved.

You can easily transfer your pictures to your PC or copy pictures from PC to your Storm as well. See Chapter 12 for more details.

Sharing your pictures

Where's the joy in taking great pictures if you're the only one seeing them? Your BlackBerry has several options for sharing your bundle of joy:

1. **In the Camera screen, press the menu key and touch-press View Pictures.**

2. **Highlight a picture you want to share.**

3. **Press the menu key.**

4. **Select from the choices listed here:**

   - *Send as Email:* This goes directly to the Compose E-Mail screen, with the currently selected picture as an attachment.

   - *Send as MMS:* Similar to Send as Email, this opens a Compose MMS screen with the currently selected picture as an attachment. The only difference is that MMS first displays Contacts, letting you select the person's phone number to receive the MMS before going to the compose screen.

   - *Send Using Bluetooth:* This allows you to send the picture to any device capable of communicating through Bluetooth.

Setting a picture as Caller ID

Wouldn't it be nice if, when your girlfriend was calling, you also could see her beautiful face? You can do that. If you have a photo of her saved in your BlackBerry, follow these steps to make sure you can:

1. **Touch-press Media icon from Home screen.**

2. **Touch-press Pictures.**

3. **Navigate to the locations of your pictures.**

4. **Touch-press to view the photo you want to appear when the person calls.**

5. **Press the menu key.**

6. **Touch-press Set as Caller ID.**

   If you don't have pictures of your friends, now's the time to start clicking.

7. **Touch-press the screen.**

   A menu appears.

8. **Touch-press Crop and Save.**

   Contacts appears.

9. **Touch-press the contact you want this picture to appear.**

   A message indicating a picture is set for that contact appears. You're set.

Setting a Home screen image

Suppose you have a stunning picture that you want to use as the background image for your BlackBerry? Follow these steps:

1. **Touch-press Media icon from Home screen.**

2. **Touch-press Pictures.**

3. **Navigate to the locations of your pictures.**

4. **Touch-press to view the picture you want to use as your Home screen image.**

5. **Press the menu key.**

6. **Touch-press Set as Home Screen Image.**

   You can always reset the Home screen image by going to the menu screen and selecting Reset Home Screen Image.

Setting Camera Memory Options

The camera in your BlackBerry is a piece of hardware and a computer program. As such, the good people at RIM (Research In Motion) incorporated some parameters that you can set so you can enjoy your camera fully while not affecting other features that share the same memory.

You should know the following two options:

- ✔ **Device Memory Limit:** The amount of device memory your camera can use. The values are 12M, 15M, 20M, and 25M (1M is 1000K). To get a feel for how many pictures this is, look at the properties of an existing picture in the format you take most often and note its file size. The size of the picture also depends on the format you use to take it.

- ✔ **Reserved Pictures Memory:** The amount of memory BlackBerry reserves for the camera to store pictures. Possible values are 0M, 2M, 5M, 8M, 10M, and 12M. You can't set this value greater than the Device Memory Limit.

Chapter 12

Satisfying Your Senses with the Media Player

*I*f a word describes today's phone market trends, it's *convergence*. Your BlackBerry Storm is one of the latest participants in this race to bring things together. We probably don't have to tell you this, but in addition to sending and receiving e-mail and being a phone, a camera, and a PDA, your BlackBerry Storm is a portable media player.

In the palm of your hand, you can

✔ Listen to music

✔ Record and watch video clips

✔ Sample ring tones

✔ Snap and view pictures

These capabilities are all bundled into an application with a name you'd recognize even after sipping a couple pints of strong ale — Media.

Accessing Media

To run Media, simply touch-press the Media icon from the Home screen. The Media icon is very easy to distinguish, as it has the image of a CD and a musical note.

Media is a collection of media applications:

- ✔ Music
- ✔ Video
- ✔ Ring tones
- ✔ Pictures
- ✔ Voice Notes

And each one is represented with an icon upon opening Media, as shown in Figure 12-1. You don't need to be Einstein to figure out what each one of these media applications is for. Ready to have some fun?

Figure 12-1:
Explore
Media here.

Music   Ring tones   Voice Notes

Video   Pictures

Let the music play

You don't need a quarter to play music on your BlackBerry Storm. Just touch-press Music from the Media screen. Several potential views of your music collection (similar to the one shown in Figure 12-2) appear. Music is the screen heading. The views include the following:

- ✓ **All Songs:** Displays all your music files in alphabetical order.

- ✓ **Artists:** Lists your music files by artist, so you can play your John Mayer songs in one go.

- ✓ **Albums:** Lets you view your music collection one album at a time.

- ✓ **Genres:** If you prefer not to mingle your country with your cutting-edge techno, navigate through this view.

- ✓ **Playlists:** Organize and play songs as you prefer — the perfect mixed tape!

- ✓ **Sample Songs:** When you're dying to check the player but haven't yet put your collection into the BlackBerry Storm, go here. Your Storm comes with a couple of songs and you can find it here.

- ✓ **Shuffle Songs:** Life is all about variety and when you're tired of the song order in your playlist, touch-press this.

After you choose a view, touch-press one of the songs to start playing it. After Storm starts playing a song, it plays the rest of the music listed in the view you selected. The standard interface shown in Figure 12-3 doesn't require explanation.

You can't fast forward or rewind the traditional way, but you can position where Storm is playing by dragging the progress slider.

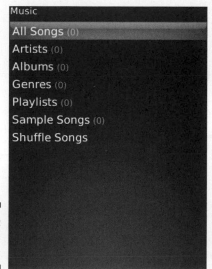

Figure 12-2:
Your music
collection.

BlackBerry Storm supports many music formats (with file extensions), including the following:

- **ACC:** Audio compression formats AAC, AAC+, and EAAC+ (`.aac` and `.m4a`)
- **AMR:** Adaptive Multi Rate-Narrow Band (AMR-NB) speech coder standard (`.mmr` and `.3gp`)
- **MIDI:** Polyphonic MIDI (`.mid`, `.midi`, and `.smf`)
- **MP3:** MPEG Part 1 and Part 2 audio layer 3 (`.mp3` and `.mp4`)
- **WMA:** Windows Media Audio 9, Pro, and 10 (`.wma` and `.asf`)

The earpiece-mic combo that comes with your BlackBerry Storm is only for one ear. This might be an issue when you're on the train. To improve your experience, you can buy a *stereo* (two-ear) headset. A Bluetooth headset is a good option.

Figure 12-3: The music plays here.

Now showing

Playing or recording a video is very similar to playing music:

1. **Touch-press Video from the Media screen.**

   The screen shows Video Camera and a list of video files on the bottom. If you want to watch a video, skip to Step 5.

2. **To start video recording, touch-press Video Camera.**

   A screen shows the image in front of the camera.

3. **Touch-press the screen again to start recording.**

   Don't wait for "Cut!" You can pause it by touch-pressing the pause button. The familiar video/audio controls appear, from left to right showing:

   - Continue recording
   - Stop
   - Play

   The functions of the other buttons are also quite obvious, including:

   - Rename (for the file name)
   - Delete
   - Send via E-Mail

4. **Press the stop button when you're ready to wrap your home video.**

   You wind up at the previous screen with the video clip file listed. We know you're itching to watch it.

5. **Touch-press the file to play it onscreen.**

Lord of the ring tones

Ah, the proliferation of ring tones; that's history. Nothing beats hearing a loud, funky ring tone while you're sleeping on a bus or a train. You can wake other passengers, too, whether you want to use the Top 40, old-fashioned digital beats, or something you recorded yourself.

Of course you want to hear ring tones that come with your BlackBerry Storm. It offers a bunch, so enjoy.

1. **Touch-press Ring Tones from the Media screen.**

   You see three views:

   - All Ring Tones
   - My Ring Tones
   - Preloaded Ring Tones

2. **Touch-press Preloaded Ring Tones.**

   The preloaded ring tones are displayed.

3. **Touch-press any one of them and enjoy.**

   While playing a ring tone, touch-press the right arrow to go to the next tone; touch-press the left arrow to go the previous one.

4. **Stumble on a ring tone you like.**

5. **Press the menu key and touch-press Set as Ring Tone.**

   That ring tone is what plays when your phone rings.

A ring tone is similar to a music file and includes the same music formats:

- ✔ ACC
- ✔ M4A
- ✔ MIDI
- ✔ MMR
- ✔ MP3
- ✔ WMA

If you're familiar with audio editing software, you can make your own ring tone. Save it as one of the formats listed above and copy it to your Storm (see the "Working with Media Files" section in this chapter to see how to copy files from your PC to your Storm). The Internet is also an amazon of ring tones, and many are free. The only possible harm you get from downloading one is being annoyed with how it sounds. The default home page on the Browser (`mobile.blackberry.com`) has links to sources of ring tones. See Fun and Pages on the home page.

Picture this

If you upgraded from an older BlackBerry, you may know Pictures, which lets you view, zoom into, and rotate pictures:

1. **Touch-press Pictures from the Media screen.**

   You see much like what you see in the other Media applications.

2. **Navigate to the view you want.**

3. **Find the picture you're looking for.**

4. Touch-press the file.

Easy does it, right?

 Check out Sample Pictures. Your BlackBerry comes with nice pictures you can use as the Home screen background. You can assign a cartoon to a contact as a Caller ID until you get a chance to take the person's picture. Or don't take the picture.

Zoom to details

Is that a pimple? No, it's not. Let's zoom in.

While viewing an image, press the menu key and touch-press Zoom. A tiny nonobtrusive slider bar appears on the left side of the image. Sliding it up zooms in and sliding it down zooms out.

While sliding, the slider bar indicates the degree of zoom. The exact center of this bar is the original image (no zooming applied).

 An image is normally defaulted to fit the screen but you can toggle it by pressing the menu key and touch-pressing one of these options:

- ✔ Fit to Screen
- ✔ View Actual Size

Rotate it

Want to view yourself upside down? Maybe not. But sometimes your pictures look better horizontal.

While you're viewing an image in Pictures, press the menu key and touch-press Rotate. The image rotates 90 degrees clockwise. By repeating the same steps, you can keep rotating it; each time is an additional 90-degree clockwise rotation.

Recording your voice

A feature-packed SmartPhone like your Storm *should* come with a voice recorder, and it does. Within Media, find Voice Notes, a neat recording application. Now you can record your billion-dollar ideas without having to type every detail:

1. **Touch-press that little microphone icon.**

   The Voice Notes application launches, sporting the simple and clean screen shown in Figure 12-4. The top of the screen is a Record button, and the bottom part lists your previous recordings.

2. **To record, touch-press Record.**

3. **When you're ready, touch-press the screen again.**

   Your BlackBerry's microphone is designed to be close to your mouth like any mobile phone should.

   You can pause anytime you want by touch-pressing the pause button. A familiar video/audio control appears, from left to right:

   • Continue recording

   • Stop

   • Play

   Other buttons include Rename for renaming the file name, Delete, and Send via E-Mail.

4. **Press the stop button to wrap it up.**

   You return to the previous screen. Your recent voice note should be listed.

5. **Touch-press your voice recording when you need to type your brilliant idea.**

Figure 12-4: Record your voice here.

Turning it up (or down)

Whether you're listening to music, watching a video, or listening to your voice recording, adjusting the volume is easy.

 Your Storm comes with dedicated volume buttons on the top-right side of the device. The top button (with the plus sign) turns the volume up, and the bottom button (with the minus sign) turns the volume down. The onscreen volume slider reflects anything you did to the volume buttons.

Navigating the menu

You can easily jump to the next item in the list. Press the menu key while you're viewing an image, listening to songs, or watching a video clip. On the menu that appears, you see the following items:

- ✔ **Next:** Jumps to the next item in the list. This appears only if an item is after this media file in the current folder.

- ✔ **Previous:** Jumps to the previous item. This appears only if a previous item is in the current folder.

- ✔ **Delete:** Deletes the media file.

- ✔ **Move:** Moves the file to a different folder.

- ✔ **Rename:** Lets you rename the media file.

- ✔ **Properties:** Displays the media file's location, size, and time of last modification.

Changing the media flavor

Like the rest of your Storm applications, you can customize things to be the way you prefer. Do it through the Options screen inside Media:

1. **Press the menu key while in Media.**

   You can press the menu key while you're in any application inside Media too.

2. **Touch-press Options.**

   The screen looks like the screen shown in Figure 12-5. You can specifically customize the Picture application and Media in general. Each is described in the following sections.

Figure 12-5:
Top of the
Media
Options
screen and
bottom of
the Media
Options
screen.

Customizing Picture

You can change the Picture application the following ways:

- **Sort By:** Allows you to toggle file sorting based on recent update or name.

- **Thumbnails Per Row:** When your files appear as a grid of *thumbnails* (small versions of your photos), this number of thumbnails is displayed per row. The higher the number, the smaller the thumbnails.

- **Slide Show Interval:** When viewing your files in a slide show, a picture appears for this many seconds before moving to the next picture.

- **Reserve Picture Memory:** Normally left to a default value, but in case you want to reserve a memory to make sure that Picture has something to use, set it here. This comes into play when you have so many applications that you're starting to run out of device memory.

- **Exclude Folders:** This is a button where you can navigate your picture folders and indicate that you don't want any of the pictures inside it displayed. This is useful for speeding up loading the list of pictures. Remember that the fewer pictures you have, the faster it is for the Picture applications to load the list. So, it isn't for your secret folders. But hey, you can use it for hiding something too.

Customizing Media

You can finesse the rest of Media:

- **Auto Stop Media Player When Idle:** The default is off but you can set it at 5, 10, 20, 30, or 45 minutes. This can save you battery life if you get distracted and you leave your BlackBerry Storm on a table playing your favorite video.

- ✔ **Turn Off Auto Backlighting:** Your Storm includes a backlight feature, which provides additional screen lighting. It turns on when you move your Storm from shade to direct sunlight. When backlighting keeps bothering you when you're watching a movie, this is the place to toggle it off. It also a good option to keep that battery juice when you badly need it.

- ✔ **Audio Boost:** You can set it On or Off.

- ✔ **Headset Equalizer:** Default to Off but if you want to have a different audio setting, you have several options here including Bass Boost, Bass Lower, Dance, Hip Hop, Jazz, Lounge, Loud, R&B, Rock, Treble Boost, Treble Lower and Vocal Boost.

- ✔ **Exclude Folders:** You don't want to display any of the pictures inside this folder. This helps make it faster to load the list of pictures. (The fewer pictures you have, the faster the Picture application can load the list.) This option isn't for your secret folders.

Working with Media Files

The ways you can get your hands on media files are evolving. Ten years back, who'd have thought that we'd be buying music from a tiny card or downloading music from an all-you-can-eat monthly subscription?

Some day, you'll wake up with a technology that doesn't require you to constantly copy media files to your handheld music player. But for now, enjoying music on the move means managing these files.

Media is a great music player, but without music files it's as useless as a guitar without strings.

Greeting BlackBerry Desktop Media Manager

Heard of Roxio? Roxio is known for its CD-*ripping,* which is a process to convert music files in CD format to other popular compressed formats. RIM licensed a portion of Roxio and packaged it with BlackBerry Desktop Software. Even though it's not the whole suite of Roxio software, it's still good news for you because you can now avail yourself of fantastic features, such as

- ✔ Ripping CDs
- ✔ Converting files to get the best playback on your BlackBerry

- Managing music files
- Syncing media files to your device

 Do you have an old version of Media Manager? No problem. Point your desktop Internet browser to na.blackberry.com/eng/services/desktop for directions on downloading the latest version for free and installing it on your PC.

In this section, we familiarize you with the Media Manager interface and then show you how to copy a video file into your BlackBerry.

Accessing Media Manager

You can get to Media Manager through BlackBerry Desktop Manager, which Chapter 14 describes in detail. Get to Desktop Manager on your PC this way:

1. **Click the Windows Start icon.**

2. **Select All Programs⇨BlackBerry⇨Desktop Manager.**

   BlackBerry Desktop Manager appears, as shown in Figure 12-6.

3. **Click the Media icon.**

   A screen displays showing Media Manager and BlackBerry Media Sync sections. Each section has a Start button.

4. **Click the Start button under the Media Manager section.**

   A screen displays showing Media Manager and BlackBerry Media Sync sections. Each section has a Start button. The initial Media Manager screen is well organized and gives you the following options:

   - Manage Pictures
   - Manage Music
   - Manage Videos
   - View Connected Devices

5. **Click one of the options.**

When you see the Media Manager screen in Figure 12-7, it may look intimidating. But it's really easy to use — plus, it follows the same interface as Windows Explorer:

- The left side is where you navigate to your folders and files.
- The right side displays the files in the folder you've currently selected on the left.

Figure 12-6:
Access
Media
Manager
here.

Figure 12-7:
View your
media files
on this
screen.

The top section looks the same as the bottom section except that the top represents your desktop, the bottom represents the BlackBerry Storm, and each are named My Media and My Devices, respectively. You can move or copy files easily. When you're copying, for example, one section can be the source, and the other section can be the destination. By simply dragging the files between the two sections, you can copy on the same screen. Neat, right?

Importing media files to Media Manager

Want a quick and easy way to import media files?

1. **Use Windows Explorer to get to the media files you want.**

2. **Drag and drop the files into Media Manager.**

You can drag and drop files to the folder in the left part of the screen, where the folder tree appears, or the right part, where the files are listed. Just make sure that when you're doing the latter, the current folder in the tree view is the folder where you want the media files to be imported.

Without using Windows Explorer, you can also use Media Manager to locate the files you want. The trick is to change the top-left side view in one of the sections to Folders. If you look closely at the top-left section, you see two tabs. The first tab, My Media, is the default view. The Folders tab has the icon of — guess what? — a folder.

Click the folder icon. You see a tree view, but this time it looks exactly as you see it in Windows Explorer, as shown in Figure 12-8. The files can be in your local hard drive or a network folder accessible by your desktop computer.

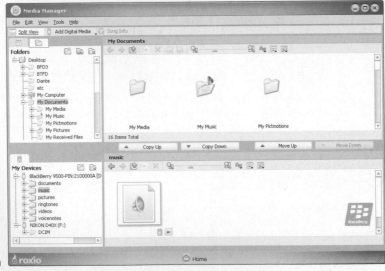

Figure 12-8:
Navigate to your desktop media files here.

Adding a media file to your BlackBerry

After you're familiar with the Media Manager, get those files copied to your BlackBerry Storm. Here's the rundown:

1. **Connect BlackBerry to your desktop computer with the USB cable that came with the device.**

Other Media Manager features

Spend some time exploring Media Manager. It has interesting features that you might find useful. Here's a quick rundown of what to expect:

✔ Import media files

✔ E-mail media files

✔ Set song info such as title, artist, album, genre, year, and an image to show as a track art when playing the song

✔ Enhance and apply special effects to photos by using PhotoSuite

✔ Record audio

✔ Customize photo printing

2. **On the Media Manager screen, drag and drop your media files from the My Media view to any folder in My Devices.**

You can drag and drop an entire album. After dropping a media file, you're prompted to convert the file into a format viewable by your BlackBerry, as shown in Figure 12-9.

3. **Choose an option:**

- *Convert for Optimal Playback:* This bet is the safest and is the default.

- *Copy with No Conversion:* Copies the file faster. The file is copied to your BlackBerry as is, but it might not play in your BlackBerry.

- *Advanced Conversion Options:* From here, another screen lets you downgrade the quality to minimize it size. Allows you to crop video so the entire screen is filled, instead of seeing dark margins.

Figure 12-9:
Choose to convert your media files for optimum playback.

Synchronizing with iTunes using BlackBerry Media Sync

If you have an iPod, you're probably using iTunes, keeping a playlist, and sub-scribing to podcasts or videocast. Podcast are downloaded to iTunes using RSS. To clarify the jargon, RSS is short for Really Simple Syndication, a kind of digital files publish-subscribe mechanism. This is the mechanism iTunes uses to receive audio and video recordings that most people refer to as podcast and videocast. Would you like to sync your BlackBerry with iTunes? Wouldn't we all? Follow these quick and easy steps to your BlackBerry Storm - iTunes synchronization:

1. **Click the Windows Start icon.**

2. **Select All Programs⇨BlackBerry⇨Desktop Manager.**

   BlackBerry Desktop Manager appears (refer to Figure 12-6).

3. **Click the Media icon.**

   A screen displays showing Media Manager and BlackBerry Media Sync sections. Each section has a Start button.

4. **Click the Start button under the BlackBerry Media Sync section.**

   A screen displays the Media Manager and BlackBerry Media Sync sections. Each section has a Start button. A pop-up screen appears just like the one shown in Figure 12-10. Note the two arrows on the bottom-left portion of the screen. Clicking those arrows gives you options of what part of iTunes you want synchronized.

5. **Click the bottom-left Show iTunes Playlist arrows.**

   A selection of what you have in iTunes shows up, as shown in Figure 12-11. This is the part of the screen where you choose iTunes media file types.

Figure 12-10:
The
BlackBerry
Media Sync
screen.

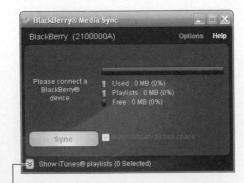

Show iTunes Playlists

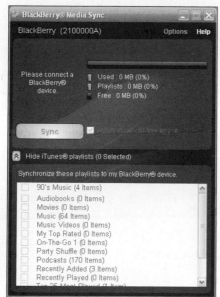

Figure 12-11:
Choose
your iTunes
media here.

6. **Select the iTunes media you want copied to your BlackBerry Storm.**

7. **Click Sync.**

There you go. You see a progress bar synchronizing the media files
from iTunes.

Downloading sounds

RIM has set up a Web site where you can download new ring tones. Simply
go to http://mobile.blackberry.com/homepage?book=ringtone_
catalog&lang=en&accept=yes and you get a screen similar to the one
shown in Figure 12-12. From this page, you can sample and download alarms,
notifiers, and tunes. And did we mention that it's free?

The ring tone plays when you select it from the three categories. After the
tune plays, you can save it by pressing the menu key and selecting Save.
RIM isn't the only site where you can find ring tones. The Web is a wonderful
place, so go hunting.

Figure 12-12:
Go here to download media files.

Transferring Media Files using the microSD

When in a hurry, running Desktop Manager and opening Media Manager can be a drag. One quick option is to copy your media files directly to microSD using the familiar Windows Explorer on your PC:

1. **Connect your Storm to your computer using the USB cable that came with your device.**

   Make sure you have the microSD in your Storm before you do this. When connected, a Storm screen displays a prompt for enabling mass storage mode.

2. **Touch-press Yes.**

   Another screen appears asking you for your password.

3. **Type your Storm password.**

   The device is now ready to behave like an ordinary flash drive. On your PC, a Removable Disk window appears which displays a couple of options to choose from.

4. **Select Open Folder to View Files, and then click OK.**

   The familiar Windows Explorer screen opens. You basically can do anything you do with a normal Windows folder. You can drag and drop, copy, and delete files.

Chapter 13

Getting around with BlackBerry GPS

A few years back when some Northern America network carriers introduced *global positioning systems (GPS)* on their version of the BlackBerry, we were quite impressed . . . until we tried it. The response time was slow, and it wasn't accurate. On top of that, the network carriers charged an arm and a leg for this inferior service. As it turns out, those GPS functions weren't actually embedded in the BlackBerry. How low tech!

Today, many BlackBerry models, including your BlackBerry Storm, come with a built-in GPS.

Depending on your network carrier, your BlackBerry Storm GPS might be disabled. For example, Verizon Wireless has a history of disabling GPS capabilities and steers users toward Verizon's own GPS application, VZ Navigator. However, an application like Google Maps uses both GPS and the network to find your location. So if GPS is disabled, Google Maps can still approximate where you are on the map.

Putting Safety First

Some GPS features are useful not only while you're walking on the street but also while you're driving a car. Although you'll be tempted to use your BlackBerry GPS while driving, we *strongly* suggest that you not adjust it while you're driving.

Before you start using BlackBerry GPS in your car, you need to get a car holder (preferably a car kit with a car charger) and to resolve the BlackBerry light issue.

You can buy a car kit online by searching for **BlackBerry car kit**. Or go to one of the following links:

- ✔ www.shopblackberry.com
- ✔ www.blackberrystuff.com/blackberry_car_kit.htm

By default, the longest your BlackBerry's backlight can stay on is two minutes, so you need something to allow your BlackBerry's backlight to stay on longer. Some GPSs let you prolong the *backlight timeout.* But a free utility called BBLight also does the job. You can get it by going to www. blackberryfordummies.com/bblight.html.

Now that you have all you need to keep you safe, keep on reading.

Getting What You Need

GPS needs *navigation maps,* which are usually downloaded in little pieces as you need them.

If you didn't subscribe to an *unlimited* data plan from your network carrier, the more you move about and use your GPS, the more map pieces you'll download, which means the more you'll have to pay.

In general, for a BlackBerry GPS to work, you need

- ✔ A BlackBerry with a built-in GPS *or* a BlackBerry with an external GPS and a Bluetooth connection (which the BlackBerry Storm has)
- ✔ A data plan from your network carrier (unlimited data plan is recommended)
- ✔ To be in an area with a radio signal (so you can download the maps)

Choosing GPS Application Options

We've identified three GPS applications that you can use on your BlackBerry:

- ✔ BlackBerry Maps
- ✔ Google Maps
- ✔ TeleNav GPS Navigator

Both BlackBerry Maps and Google Maps are free.

BlackBerry Maps

Out of the box, your BlackBerry comes with the BlackBerry Maps application. See Figure 13-1.

You can use BlackBerry Maps to do the following:

✔ Find a location by typing an address or by using Contacts

✔ Get point-to-point directions (from an airport to a hotel, for instance)

✔ E-mail or SMS a location to colleagues and friends

✔ Turn GPS on or off

✔ Zoom in and out of the map

You can turn GPS on or off. You can still perform these functions with it turned off, but you won't see where you're actually located.

You can tweak the light setting in BlackBerry Maps:

1. **Press the menu key and touch-press Maps.**

2. **Press the menu key and touch-press Options.**

3. **In the Backlight Timeout When field, touch-press < 50% Battery.**

   You can set this to whatever you like, but we recommend <50% or <25% for this field.

4. **Press menu key and touch-press Save.**

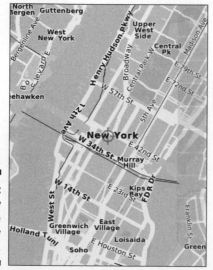

Figure 13-1:
BlackBerry
Maps on the
BlackBerry
Storm.

Google Maps

Google Maps is the mobile version of maps.google.com. It has most of the online features, including satellite imaging and traffic information. Best of all, it's free.

Like BlackBerry Map, you can use Google Maps even without a GPS, but it gets better. You can search for businesses and landmarks, just as you do on maps.google.com. It's like having the ultimate 411 (with a map) at the tip of your fingers.

Because Google Maps doesn't come with your BlackBerry, you need to download it.

1. **Open your BlackBerry Storm Browser.**

2. **Go to** www.google.com/gmm.

   The Web page loads and its icon appears on your Home screen.

3. **After Google Maps is loaded, press the menu key.**

   The menu shown in Figure 13-2 opens. From here you can do the following:

   - Find businesses and landmarks, including phone numbers, street addresses, and Web addresses

   - Find and map exact addresses

   - Get step-by-step directions from point A to point B

   - View satellite images of the current map (shown in the left of Figure 13-3)

   - Get traffic information for major highways

With GPS on, your current location is a blue blinking dot. The right part of Figure 13-3 shows this dot.

You can use these Google Maps shortcuts:

- ✔ **Zoom in:** I key

- ✔ **Zoom out:** O key (That's the letter O.)

- ✔ **Go to the current location:** 0 key (That's the number 0.)

You need to have a radio signal to download maps to your BlackBerry Storm. In addition, we recommend having an unlimited data plan if you use the GPS a lot.

Figure 13-2:
Google
Maps menu.

Figure 13-3:
Google
Maps
showing
a satellite
photo (left)
and the cur-
rent location
(right).

TeleNav GPS Navigator

TeleNav GPS Navigator is a full-featured GPS solution; it's a GPS *device replacement,* which means the folks at TeleNav want you to use your BlackBerry in the car. Unlike the other products listed earlier, TeleNav has turn-by-turn voice instructions to get you to your destination.

At the time of this writing, TeleNav hadn't fixed the backlight timeout issue. This means that about every two minutes, you must press a key on your BlackBerry to keep the light on.

TeleNav's feature list is extensive and includes these:

- 3D maps; see Figure 13-4
- Real-time compass
- Wi-Fi hotspot finder

The list goes on and on. The feature we like the most is the human-voice step-by-step driving directions.

The extensive features come at a price. Depending on your network carrier, TeleNav costs about $10 a month and offers a 60-day free trial. Visit www. telenav.com for more information. After the product is downloaded, an icon appears on your screen.

Figure 13-4: TeleNav offers a 3D map while you drive.

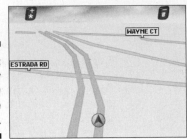

Part IV
Working with Desktop Manager

The 5th Wave   By Rich Tennant

"Most of our product line is doing well, but the expanding touch pad on our PDA keeps opening unexpectedly."

In this part . . .

Here you discover essential information about some behind-the-scenes-yet-integral processes. Read all about Desktop Manager, which you direct to monitor and control database synchronization (Chapter 14), and how to leverage Device Switch Wizard to migrate your existing data to your new BlackBerry (Chapter 15). You also find how to back up your data (Chapter 16) and the many ways of installing applications (Chapter 17) to your BlackBerry Storm.

Chapter 14

Syncing the Synchronize Way

. . . .

In This Chapter

▶ Introducing BlackBerry Desktop Manager

▶ Preparing your PC for PIM synchronization

▶ Using manual and automatic synchronization

. . . .

What better way to keep your BlackBerry Storm updated than to *synchronize* or reconcile it with your desktop application's data?

Arguably, most of the data you need to synchronize is from your *Personal Information Manager (PIM)* applications: notes, appointments, addresses, and tasks. The crucial piece for data synchronization to and from your device and desktop computer is Synchronize. This third-party software allows you to synchronize as well as upload and download media files between your PC and BlackBerry.

In this chapter, we introduce Synchronize. We show you how to manually and automatically synchronize your BlackBerry Storm with your desktop computer. We also offer tips for which options you might want to use. Before we get into all that, however, we include a section on BlackBerry Desktop Manager.

Meeting Your BlackBerry Desktop Manager

The centerpiece of the desktop activities that you can do with your BlackBerry Storm is *BlackBerry Desktop Manager (BDM),* which is a suite of programs that include the following:

✔ **Application Loader:** Installs BlackBerry applications and updates the BlackBerry OS.

✔ **Backup and Restore:** Backs up your BlackBerry data and settings. Check out Chapter 16 for details.

✔ **Synchronize:** Synchronizes BlackBerry data to your PC (a topic of this chapter).

✔ **Media Manager:** Uploads media files to your BlackBerry Storm from your PC and vice versa (another topic in this chapter).

BDM is the software included on the CD that comes with your handheld device. Your BlackBerry Storm's packaging tells you how to install BDM on your desktop computer.

Installing BDM and Desktop Redirector

The CD that comes with your BlackBerry Storm allows you to install BDM. At the same time, you can install Desktop Redirector. When you insert the CD, the installation wizard automatically runs. Follow the wizard. One of the screens on the wizard allows you to choose whether this installation is for personal or for work e-mail. Choosing for work actually allows you to use e-mail for both personal and work using the Desktop Redirector.

Desktop Redirector allows you to redirect e-mail that you receive on your Outlook. This means even if you get your e-mails through Outlook, you can have those e-mails redirected to your personal BlackBerry.

If you want to redirect your Outlook e-mail to your BlackBerry, when you're installing BDM, make sure you click Desktop Redirector in the installation screen, as shown in Figure 14-1.

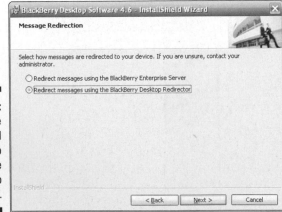

Figure 14-1:
Configure
the BDM
install to
include
Desktop
Redirector.

Launching BDM

In most Windows installations, you find the shortcut to launch BDM through your computer's Start menu:

1. **Choose Start⇨All Programs⇨BlackBerry⇨Desktop Manager.**

2. **Connect your Storm to your computer using the USB cable that came with your device.**

   When you connect your Storm to a PC, your Storm screen displays a prompt for enabling mass storage mode. It also asks for your Storm password. In mass storage mode, your Storm behaves like a flash drive. A new drive is added to My Computer in Windows Explorer, which allows you to treat the microSD in your Storm as a normal flash drive.

3. **Launch BDM.**

   The BDM opening screen appears; see Figure 14-2.

BDM installation can vary from phone provider to provider. At the very least, you should see at least four icons or applications:

- ✔ Application Loader (Chapter 17)
- ✔ Backup and Restore (Chapter 16)
- ✔ Media (see Chapter 12)
- ✔ Synchronize

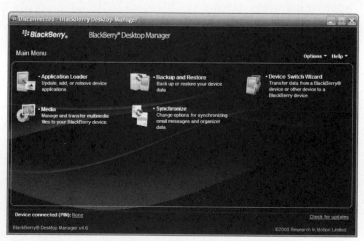

Figure 14-2:
BlackBerry
Desktop
Manager.

Connecting BDM to your Storm

You establish a connection between your BlackBerry Storm and BDM through the USB cable that comes with your device.

Before you start connecting BDM to your BlackBerry Storm, find out what your BlackBerry Storm PIN is. You can find out your PIN in Chapter 8.

Follow these steps to connect your BlackBerry to BDM:

1. **Plug in your device to your desktop.**

2. **Launch BDM.**

   When BDM is running, it tries to find a BlackBerry on the type of connection specified. The default connection is USB, so you shouldn't need to configure anything.

3. **If your device has a password, BDM prompts for the password.**

4. **Enter the password.**

   You see Connected as the screen heading. If for some reason you see Disconnected and no password prompt, one of the following is happening:

   • BDM can't find the device being connected via the USB cable.

   • The connection setting isn't set to use USB.

5. **Choose Options⇨Connection Options at the side of the BDM screen.**

   The screen shown in Figure 14-3 appears. Make sure that the connection setting uses USB.

6. **In the Connection Type drop-down list, select the USB connection with your BlackBerry Storm's PIN.**

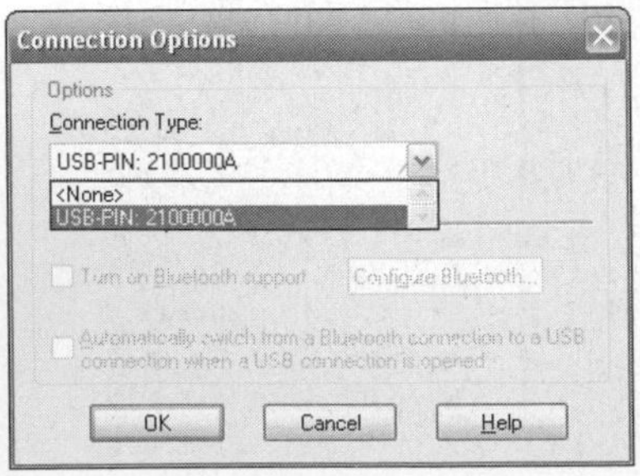

Figure 14-3: Possible connection types to your BlackBerry Storm.

Connection Options
Options
Connection Type:
USB-PIN: 2100000A
<None>
USB-PIN: 2100000A
Turn on Bluetooth support   Configure Bluetooth...
Automatically switch from a Bluetooth connection to a USB connection when a USB connection is opened
OK   Cancel   Help

Running BDM for the first time

If you're running BDM for the first time, the program does these things:

- ✔ Tries to make the initial configuration on your machine, which includes security encryption setup. It asks you to randomly move your mouse to generate security encryption keys.

- ✔ Checks what applications you have on your device and what required applications need to be installed. If it can't find a required application on your device, it prompts you to install it. Of course, you have the option to cancel and install later.

- ✔ Looks at the settings you have for your Synchronize software. If auto-synchronization is turned on, BDM attempts to run synchronization for your PIM. This is discussed later, in the "Synchronizing automatically" section.

Setting Up Synchronize

Synchronize is the part of BDM that allows you to coordinate your data between your desktop computer and your BlackBerry Storm. Synchronize is one of the icons on the BlackBerry Desktop Manager screen. To launch the program, simply double-click the Synchronize icon. A screen appears like the one in Figure 14-4.

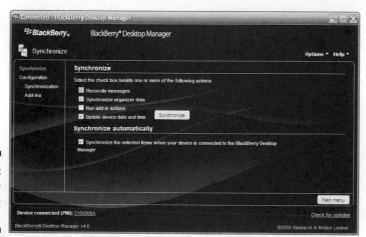

Figure 14-4:
The
Synchronize
screen.

The Synchronize screen is divided into two sections, which you can navigate through the left links:

✔ **Synchronize** is the default view and allows you to manually trigger synchronization. See Figure 14-4. See the "Using On-Demand Synchronize" and "Synchronizing automatically" sections later in this chapter for more details and for when you use this screen.

✔ **Configuration** is where you can set up configuration and rules for reconciling data. Within this are two subsections, Synchronization and Add-ins. These further organize the interface. See Figure 14-5. The first thing you need to figure out is the Synchronization subsection. The next section helps you do that.

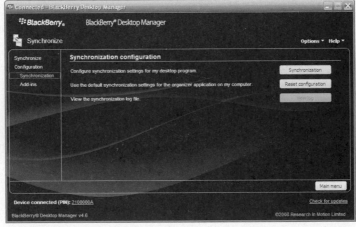

Figure 14-5: The Configuration screen.

Configuring PIM synchronization

Notice this important item in the Synchronization configuration subsection, as shown in Figure 14-5: the Synchronization button. You use that button to configure PIM (personal information manager) synchronization.

PIM info includes the following:

✔ Calendar

✔ MemoPad

✔ Address Book

✔ Tasks

Clicking the Synchronization button displays the screen in Figure 14-6. You can see that names correspond to the Storm applications except for Contacts, which goes by Address Book. This is the entry point of the entire synchronization configuration for PIM applications. Selecting the application on this screen allows you to pair the PIM handheld application to a desktop application; Outlook in this example.

The PIM Configuration screen allows you to select which application data you want to sync with your Blackberry. The following popular PIM applications can be synched to your Storm: ACT!, ASCII Text File Converter, Lotus Notes, Lotus Organizer, Microsoft Outlook, Microsoft Outlook Express, and Microsoft Schedule.

Here are the four types of application data that can be synchronized to your Blackberry:

- ✔ **Calendar** can be selected if you want to synchronize your appointments and events stored in your favorite PIM application.

- ✔ **MemoPad** can be selected if you want to synchronize any notes or text that you may have been storing in your PIM application.

- ✔ **Address Book** can be selected if you want to synchronize any contact information into your Storm.

- ✔ **Tasks** can be selected if you want to synchronize your to-do list.

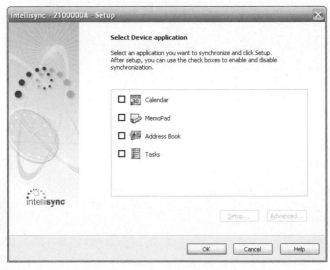

Figure 14-6:
The PIM Configuration screen.

Follow these steps to set up your device's synchronization:

1. **Connect your Storm to BDM.**

2. **Click the Synchronize icon.**

3. **In the Configuration section, select Synchronization.**

   In the Synchronization Configuration section, you see a Configure Synchronization Settings for my Desktop Program label. Click the Synchronization button beside this label, and the PIM configuration screen is displayed.

4. **Choose an application data type (such as Calendar, MemoPad, Address Book, and Tasks) to synchronize.**

   Highlight an application data type (in this example, we selected the Calendar application data type) and click the Setup button. This brings up Calendar Setup screen.

5. **Select a PIM application to retrieve application data from by highlighting your desired application.**

   BDM pulls your selected application data from the application selected from this screen (in Figure 14-7, we selected Microsoft Outlook). This means when you synchronize your Storm, the BDM retrieves Calendar data from Microsoft Outlook.

6. **Click the Next button.**

   The Synchronization Options screen appears (see Figure 14-8).

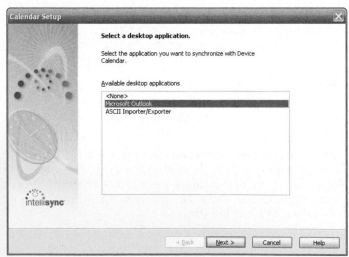

Figure 14-7:
Choose the desktop application here.

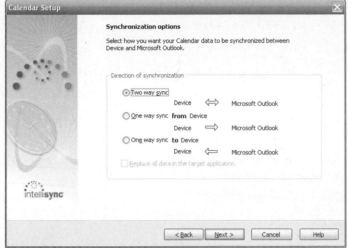

Figure 14-8:
Decide
which
direction
synchro-
nization
follows
here.

7. **In the Synchronization Options screen, select which direction the synchronization will follow.**

   Here are the three synchronization direction options available:

   • *Two Way Sync* allows you to synchronize changes both in your Storm and in your desktop application.

   • *One Way Sync from Device* synchronizes only the changes made to your Storm. Changes to your desktop application aren't reflected in your Blackberry.

   • *One Way Sync to Device* synchronizes changes made in your desktop application to your Storm. Any changes made in your Storm aren't reflected in your desktop application.

8. **Click the Next button.**

   The Options screen opens for the PIM application you selected in Step 5. Figure 14-9 shows the Microsoft Outlook Options screen (see Figure 14-9).

   For synchronization to Microsoft Outlook, make sure you're selecting the correct user profile in the Outlook User Profile drop-down list. This is particularly pertinent in cases where you have multiple user profiles in your computer. Choosing the wrong one may result in your putting the wrong data into your Storm.

   The amount of data that is reconciled or synchronized on a given application can also be controlled. For example, as shown in Figure 14-9, the last portion of the configuration allows you to specify whether to transfer all Calendar items or just a set of appointments according to dates.

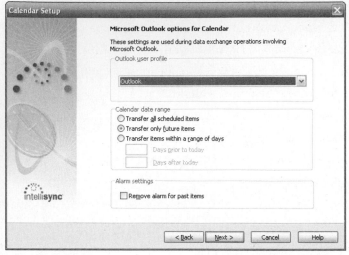

Figure 14-9:
Specific
application
settings can
be selected
in this
screen.

9. **Click the Next button.**

   This brings you to the Calendar Setup Finish screen. You can just click the Finish button to complete configuring the Calendar synchronization you've selected.

Mapping fields for synchronization

For all four PIM applications, Synchronize is intelligent enough to know what information, such as names, phone numbers, and addresses in Contacts, corresponds to Outlook. These bits of information or attributes are referred to as a *field*. For instance, the value of a home phone number field in a contact needs to be mapped to the corresponding field in Outlook so that information is transferred correctly.

But not all fields on the desktop side exist on the handheld (and vice versa). For example, a Nick Name field doesn't exist in the BlackBerry Contacts but is available on Exchange (Outlook) Address Book. In some instances, Synchronization provides an alternate field and lets you decide whether to map.

If you ever find the need to change the default mapping, you can. The interface is the same for all PIM applications. To illustrate how to map and un-map fields, we use Address Book.

The following steps lead you to the screen that allows you to map the fields for Address Book:

1. **From BDM, click Synchronize.**

2. **Click Synchronization from the Configuration subsection link.**

3. **Click the Synchronization button.**

   The PIM Configuration screen appears (refer to Figure 14-6).

4. **Click Address Book to highlight.**

   The Advanced button is enabled.

5. **Click the Advanced button.**

   The Advanced screen opens, as shown in Figure 14-10.

6. **Click the Map Fields button.**

   The Map Fields screen for Address Book/Contacts application appears; see Figure 14-11. To map or un-map, click the arrow keys.

   If you're not careful, you can inadvertently unclick Job Title mapping, and suddenly titles aren't in sync. Double-check your mapping before you click the OK button. If you think you made a mistake, you can click Cancel to save yourself from having to restore settings.

7. **Click OK to save your changes.**

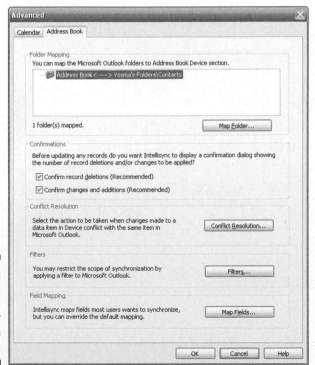

Figure 14-10:
The
Advanced
screen for
Address
Book.

Figure 14-11:
The Map
Fields
screen for
Address
Book.

Confirming record changes

Face facts: Doing a desktop synchronization isn't very interesting, and few people perform it on a regular basis.

You can tell Synchronize to prompt you for any changes it's trying to make (or perhaps undo) on either side of the wire. The Advanced screen comes in here. To get to this view, follow these steps:

1. **From BDM, double-click Synchronize.**

   The Synchronize screen appears.

2. **Click Synchronization from the Configuration subsection link.**

3. **Click the Synchronization button.**

   The PIM configuration screen appears; refer to Figure 14-6.

4. **Click Address Book to highlight.**

   If you want a PIM application other than Address Book, click that application from the list.

5. **Click the Advanced button.**

   The Advanced screen for Address Book screen appears; refer to Figure 14-10. This screen has a Confirmations section and gives you two options:

   • Confirm Record Deletions (Recommended)

   • Confirm Changes and Additions (Recommended)

   Regardless of whether you select the first option, Synchronize displays a prompt if it detects that it's about to delete *all* records.

Resolving update conflicts

Synchronize needs to know how you want to handle any conflicts between your BlackBerry and desktop application. A conflict normally happens when the same record is updated in the BlackBerry and also in Outlook. For instance, you change Jane Doe's mobile number in Storm and also change her mobile number in Outlook. Where you resolve these conflicts is the same for all PIM applications. Again, for illustration, we use Address Book as an example:

1. **From BDM, double-click Synchronize.**

   The Synchronize screen appears.

2. **Click Synchronization from the Configuration subsection link.**

3. **Click the Synchronization button.**

   The PIM configuration screen appears; refer to Figure 14-6.

4. **Click Address Book to highlight.**

   If you want a PIM application other than Address Book, select that application from the list.

5. **Click the Advanced button.**

   The Advanced Settings for Address Book screen appears; refer to Figure 14-10. This screen has five sections, and the third section is Conflict Resolution. And on this section, note the Conflict Resolution button.

6. **Click the Conflict Resolution button.**

   The Conflict Resolution screen is shown in Figure 14-12.

   You can tell Synchronize to handle conflicts in a few ways. Here are the options shown in the Address Book Advanced Settings screen:

   • *Add All Conflicting Items:* When a conflict happens, add a new record to the BlackBerry for the changes on the desktop and add a new record to the desktop for the changes on the BlackBerry.

Figure 14-12: Manage conflicts here.

- *Ignore All Conflicting Items:* Ignores the change and keeps the data the same on both sides.

- *Notify Me When Conflict Occur:* This option is the safest. Synchronize displays the details of the conflict and lets you resolve it.

- *Device Wins:* Unless you're sure this is the case, you shouldn't choose this option. It tells Synchronize to disregard the changes in the desktop and use handheld changes every time it encounters a conflict.

- *Microsoft Outlook Wins:* If you're not using MS Outlook, this option is based on your application. This option tells Synchronize to always discard changes on the handheld and use the desktop application change whenever it encounters a conflict. Again, we don't recommend this option because there's no telling on which side you made the good update.

7. **Click the option you want.**

8. **Click OK to save the settings.**

Ready, Set, Synchronize!

Are you ready to synchronize? Earlier in this chapter, we show you how to define synchronization filters and rules for your e-mail and PIM data. Now it's time to be brave and push the button. You can synchronize one of two ways:

- Manually (by clicking the Synchronize Now icon)
- Automatically (by choosing How Often on the calendar)

Using On-Demand Synchronize

This portion of Synchronize is a feature that lets you run synchronization manually. Remember that even if you set up automatic synchronization, actual synchronization doesn't happen right away. So, if you made updates to your appointments in Outlook while your Storm is connected to your PC, this feature allows you to be sure that your updates made it to your Storm before heading out the door.

Without delay, here are the steps:

1. **From BDM, double-click Synchronize.**

    The Synchronize screen appears; refer to Figure 14-4. The following four check boxes let you be selective:

- *Reconcile Messages:* E-mail.

- *Synchronize Organizer Data:* Includes notes, appointments, addresses, and tasks.

- *Run Add-In Actions:* This option comes to play when you have third-party applications that require data synchronization between your PC and your Storm.

- *Update Device Date and Time:* You only need it if you want both PC and Storm to have the same time. This ensures that you're reminded of your appointments at the same time for both Outlook and Storm.

2. **Select the check boxes of the data you want synchronized.**

3. **Click the Synchronize button.**

   Synchronize starts running the synchronization, and you see a progress screen. If you set up prompts for conflicts and Synchronize encounters one, a screen appears so you can resolve it. When finished, the progress screen disappears, and the Synchronize screen reappears.

   If you've turned on automatic synchronization (see the next section), the items you select in Step 2 automatically sync every time you connect your BlackBerry Storm to your PC.

4. **Click the Close button.**

Synchronizing automatically

How many times do you think you reconfigure your Synchronize setup? Rarely, right? After you have it configured, that's it. And if you're like us, the reason you open BlackBerry Desktop Manager is because you want to run Synchronize. Opening Synchronize and clicking the Synchronize Now button is somewhat annoying.

If you want to make Synchronize run automatically every time you connect your BlackBerry Storm to your PC, simply make sure you select the very last check box in Figure 14-4 — Synchronize the Items When Your Device is Connected to the BlackBerry Desktop Manager.

You might be asking what items auto-synchronization synchs? Good question. The items you've checked in the top portion of Figure 14-4.

Chapter 15

Switching Devices

Wouldn't it be nice if you could just make one device's data available to another? That's the future. But right now, RIM wants to make switching devices as painless as possible. That's why an application called Device Switch Wizard is part of the suite of applications in BlackBerry Desktop Manager.

Switching to BlackBerry Storm

Switching from an older BlackBerry to your BlackBerry Storm is no big deal. When you want to transfer application data (e-mails and contacts, for example) to your new Storm, the BlackBerry Desktop Manager's Device Switch Wizard backs up your old BlackBerry and loads that backup to your new device.

1. **On your PC, choose Start⇨Programs⇨BlackBerry⇨Desktop Manager.**

   The Desktop Manager screen opens, where you can find Device Switch Wizard, as shown in Figure 15-1.

2. **Click the Device Switch Wizard icon.**

   The Device Switch Wizard screen lets you choose whether to switch from BlackBerry to BlackBerry or from non-BlackBerry to BlackBerry. On the BlackBerry to BlackBerry section, it tells you to connect your current (old) BlackBerry to your PC.

Figure 15-1:
Launch
Device
Switch
Wizard
here.

3. **Connect your old BlackBerry to your PC with the USB cable.**

4. **Click the Start button below the Switch BlackBerry devices.**

   The next screen lets you verify the PINs for both devices, the old BlackBerry in the left and your Storm in the right, as shown in Figure 15-2. Because you only connected your old BlackBerry, it should be preselected.

   Your BlackBerry PIN isn't a password, but your BlackBerry SmartPhone identifier. You can find your BlackBerry PIN by going to Options⇨ Status.

5. **Decide whether to include user data and third-party applications and click the Next button.**

   If you want all the data, leave the screen untouched; this backs up everything. *Third-party applications* are all the programs you installed — the ones that didn't come with the device originally.

   Some older BlackBerry applications cater to keyboard, trackwheel, and trackballs, and might not work on the Storm. At first, *include user data only,* not third-party applications.

   A status screen appears, showing the progress of the backup operation. When the backup is finished, the next screen prompts you for the PIN of your Storm.

Figure 15-2:
Verify that
your old
BlackBerry
is con-
nected to
the PC and
decide data
to include
here.

6. **Connect your new BlackBerry Storm to your PC with the micro-USB cable.**

   The next screen, shown in Figure 15-3, lets you verify that your Storm is connected properly with the PIN displayed. It also asks you for the password.

Figure 15-3:
Type your
device
password
here.

7. **Enter the password of your Storm and click the OK button.**

   A screen similar to Figure 15-4 tells you what will be restored to the new device. Nothing has been done to your Storm yet, and this is your last chance to cancel the process.

8. **Click the Finish button.**

   A progress screen shows you the loading process.

9. **When the Success screen appears, click the Close button.**

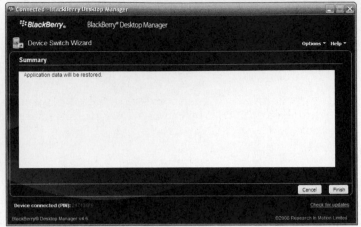

Figure 15-4:
Confirming
the loading
of data to
your new
BlackBerry.

Switching from a Non-BlackBerry Device

Device Switch Wizard supports two types of non-BlackBerry devices:

- ✔ Palm
- ✔ Microsoft Windows Mobile

This doesn't mean that you can't import your old data if you have another device. The Device Switch Wizard just makes it simpler for these two types of devices. Check out Chapter 14 for synchronization options to your Desktop PIM application if your old device is neither Palm nor Microsoft Windows Mobile.

Palm device requirements

Your equipment has to meet three prerequisites for Device Switch Wizard to import data from Palm to BlackBerry:

- ✔ Your PC must be running Windows 2000 or later.
- ✔ One of the following Palm Desktop software versions must be installed on your desktop:
  - • 4.0.1
  - • 4.1

- 4.1.4
- 6.0.1

↳ The Palm Desktop software installed is synchronizing properly with the Palm device.

You can check your Palm user guide for more details about your Palm device and on synchronizing it to PC. You can also download the user guide from www.palm.com/us/support/downloads.

Windows Mobile device requirements

You need the following things for the wizard to work properly with a Windows Mobile device:

↳ Your PC must be running Windows 2000 or later.

↳ One of the following Microsoft ActiveSync versions must be installed on your PC:

- 4.0.1
- 4.1
- 4.1.4
- 6.0.1

↳ The Mobile device must run one of the following operating systems:

- Microsoft Windows Mobile 2000, 2002, 2003, 2003SE, or 2005/5.0 for Pocket PC
- Microsoft Windows Mobile SmartPhone software 2002, 2003, or 2003 SE

Running the wizard

Before you run the wizard, make sure that all the requirements for your device are in place. We also recommend hot-syncing or synchronizing your Palm or Windows Mobile device; this ensures that the data you're sending to your BlackBerry is current. Palm Desktop software as well as the Microsoft ActiveSync should come with help information on how to hot-sync.

Although the following steps migrate Windows Mobile data into the BlackBerry, the steps are similar for Palm as well. We indicate at what point the steps vary. Do the following to get your other device's data migrated over to your new BlackBerry:

1. **Connect both the Windows Mobile device and the BlackBerry Storm to your desktop computer.**

2. **On your PC, choose Start➪Programs➪BlackBerry➪Desktop Manager.**

   The Desktop Manager screen appears; refer to Figure 15-1.

3. **Click the Device Switch Wizard icon.**

   The Device Switch Wizard screen appears.

4. **Click the image next to Switch from another Device to BlackBerry Device.**

   The welcome screen, as shown in Figure 15-5, describes what the tool can do.

5. **Click the Next button.**

   A screen prompts you to decide whether you're migrating from Palm or Windows Mobile, as shown in Figure 15-6. The wizard is intelligent enough to enable the option associated to the connected device, which in this case is the Windows Mobile device.

Figure 15-5: Migrating data from a non-BlackBerry device.

Figure 15-6: The wizard has already selected which device to port.

6. **Click the Next button.**

   Hot-syncing of Windows Mobile device kicks in at this point. You see a series of screens appearing for each of the device data. A sample of it for the Calendar data is shown in Figure 15-7. Nothing comes of it if you already performed a hot-sync before running the wizard; otherwise, it will take some time depending on how much data it has to sync between the device and the desktop software.

7. **Click OK.**

   A progress screen appears. Before the data is applied to your BlackBerry Storm, the wizard prompts you about the change, as shown in Figure 15-8. Click the following buttons on this screen to either confirm or reject the change:

   - *Details:* Click this if you want to know the records the wizard is trying to apply.

   - *Accept:* Click this if you just want the data migrated.

   - *Reject:* Allows you to ignore this data and continue.

   - *Cancel:* If you change your mind and cancel the whole operation.

8. **Click the Accept or Reject button on any confirmation screens that appear.**

   The wizard migrates all the data you accepted. When the migration process is finished, a success screen appears.

9. **Click the Finish button.**

Figure 15-7: A message showing hot-syncing on your device.

Figure 15-8: Confirm the importing of data here.

Chapter 16

Protecting Your Information

. . . .

. . . .

*I*magine that you left your beautiful BlackBerry Storm in the back of a cab. You've lost your Storm for good. Okay, not good. What happens to all your information? How are you going to replace all those contacts? What about security?

One thing that you *don't* need to worry about is information security — *if* you set up a security password on your BlackBerry. With security password protection on your Storm, anyone who finds your Storm has only ten chances to enter the correct password; after those ten chances are up, it's self-destruction time. Although it isn't as smoky as *Mission Impossible,* your BlackBerry Storm does erase all its information, thwarting your would-be data thief.

Set up a password for your Storm *now!* For information on how to do so, see Chapter 3.

Now, how to get back all the information that was on your BlackBerry Storm? If you're like us and store important information on your BlackBerry, this chapter is for you. Vital information, such as clients' and friends' contact information, notes from phone calls with clients — and, of course, those precious e-mail messages — shouldn't be taken lightly. Backing up this information is a reliable way to protect it from being lost forever.

If your BlackBerry is not in a BlackBerry Enterprise Server, which is typically the case when you work for a large corporation, BlackBerry Desktop Manager is the only way to back up and restore information to and from your desktop PC. But in the recent months, SmrtGuard has come up with a wireless backup and restore service for those who don't have the habit of plugging their

BlackBerry into their PC. If that's you, go to the end of this chapter where we introduce SmrtGuard's backup and restore solution that will give you peace of mind when it comes to protecting your data.

Accessing Backup and Restore

Backup and Restore is a BlackBerry Desktop Manager (BDM) application. It allows you to back up all the sensitive data on your BlackBerry, including contacts, e-mails, memos, to-dos, all personal preferences and options, and more.

Note: For most of you, your e-mails are already stored in accounts, such as Gmail or Yahoo! mail. But some still like to back up e-mails just in case.

1. **Install BDM on your PC.**

   For instructions on installing BDM, see Chapter 14.

2. **Connect your Storm to your PC with the USB cable that came with your BlackBerry.**

   If everything is set up right, a pop-up window on your PC asks you to type your BlackBerry security password.

3. **Type your password.**

   The BlackBerry connects to the PC.

4. **Double-click the Backup and Restore icon on the BlackBerry Desktop Manager screen.**

   The Backup and Restore screen opens; see Figure 16-1. You're ready to back up data from or restore information to your BlackBerry.

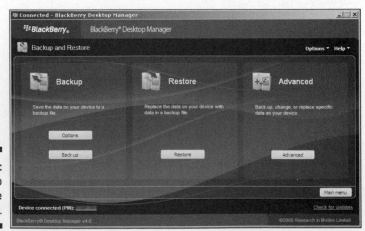

Figure 16-1: The Backup and Restore screen.

Backing Up BlackBerry Style

We all know that backing up your data provides tremendous peace of mind. So do the folks at RIM, which is why backing up your information is quite easy. You can back up your BlackBerry Storm manually or by autopilot.

Backing up your Storm manually

To back up your BlackBerry Storm on demand, follow these steps:

1. **From the BDM screen, double-click the Backup and Restore icon.**

   The Backup and Restore screen appears; refer to Figure 16-1.

2. **Click the Backup button.**

   The dialog box shown in Figure 16-2 appears, so you can name the backup file and figure out where on your PC you want to save it.

3. **Name your backup file and choose a place to save it.**

4. **Select Save.**

   BDM starts backing up your BlackBerry information onto your PC. Figure 16-3 shows the backup progress in the Transfer in Progress window.

   Don't unplug your BlackBerry Storm from the PC until the backup is finished! The folks at RIM have made the USB transfer fast, so you don't have to wait that long!

5. **When the Transfer in Progress window disappears, you can unplug the BlackBerry from the PC.**

Figure 16-2:
Decide where to save your backup file.

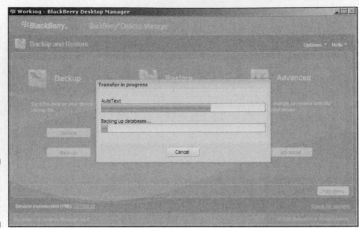

Figure 16-3:
A backup is
in progress.

Setting up automatic backups

What's better than backing up your information once? Remembering to back up regularly! What's better than backing up regularly? You guessed it — running backups automatically. After you schedule automated BlackBerry backups, you can really have peace of mind when it comes to preventing information loss.

Follow these steps to set up an autobackup:

1. **From the BDM, double-click the Backup and Restore icon.**

   The Backup and Restore screen appears.

2. **Click the Options button.**

   The Backup and Restore Options screen appears, where you can schedule automatic backups. See Figure 16-4.

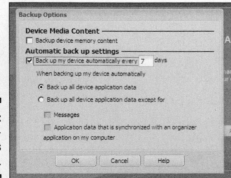

Figure 16-4:
Set auto-
backups
here.

3. **Select the Back Up My Device Automatically Every option.**

   This lets you make more decisions (check boxes and options become active), such as how often you want BDM to back up your BlackBerry.

4. **In the Days field, select a number of days between 1 and 99.**

   This interval sets how often your BlackBerry Storm is backed up. For example, if you enter **14**, your Storm is backed up every 14 days.

5. **Select the Backup All Device Application Data option.**

   This option backs up all the data on your BlackBerry Storm each time autobackup runs.

   Although you can exclude e-mail messages and information, such as from Contacts, to-do's, and memos, we recommend that you back up _everything_ each time.

6. **Click OK.**

   Now you can go on with your life without worrying when to back up.

To run a backup, your BlackBerry Storm must be connected to your PC. Make sure you plug your Storm into your PC once in a while so autobackup has a chance to back up your information.

Restoring Your Data from Backup Information

We hope that you never have to read this section more than once. A _full restore_ means bringing back all your information from a backup. It probably means you've lost information that you had hoped to find from the backup you created on your PC.

The steps to fully restoring your backup information are simple:

1. **From the BDM, double-click the Backup and Restore icon.**

   The Backup and Restore screen appears.

2. **Click the Restore button.**

   An Open File dialog box asks where the backup file is on your PC.

3. **Choose a backup file and click Open.**

   A warning window appears when you're about to do a full restore (see Figure 16-5), alerting you that you're about to overwrite existing information.

Backup and Restore

The data in the following databases will replace the current data on your device. Do you wish to proceed?

Database	Records	Bytes
Browser Urls	10	573
MMS Messages		
Phone Options	1	380
Browser Options	1	228
Browser Messages		
Messenger Options (Ya...	1	33
Browser Channels		
Browser Push Options	1	71
PasswordKeeper Options	1	65
Camera Options	1	126
Smart Card Options	1	37

Yes   No

Figure 16-5: Be careful when overwriting existing info.

4. **Click OK to go ahead with the full restore.**

   A progress bar appears.

   It might take a while for the full restore to finish. Don't unplug your BlackBerry Storm from your PC during this time!

5. **When the progress bar disappears, unplug the device from the PC.**

Protecting Your Data, Your Way

A certain burger joint and BlackBerry have in common that you can have it *your way* with their products. Just like you can get your burger with or without all the extras (such as pickles and onions), you can choose to not back up and restore things that you know you won't need.

For example, say you've accidentally deleted all your Internet bookmarks and now you want them back. *Don't* restore all the information from your last backup. That could be more than 90 days ago (depending on how often your autobackup runs, if at all). You might unintentionally overwrite other information, such as e-mail or new contacts. You want to restore bookmarks only.

If you lose something in particular, or want something specific back on your BlackBerry, use the selective backup and restore function in BDM and restore only what you need. The same goes with backing up. If you're a big e-mail user, back up *just* your e-mails and nothing else.

In this section, we use the term *databases*. Don't worry; this isn't as technical as you think. Think of a database as an information category on the BlackBerry. For example, saying, "backing up your Browser bookmarks database" is just a fancy way of saying, "backing up all your Browser bookmarks on your BlackBerry."

We start with a selective backup and then describe a selective restore.

Backing up, your way

To back up specific information, follow these steps:

1. **From the BDM, double-click the Backup and Restore icon.**

   The Backup and Restore screen appears.

2. **Click the Advanced button.**

   The advanced Backup and Restore screen appears, as shown in Figure 16-6. The right side of the screen shows different information categories, or *databases*.

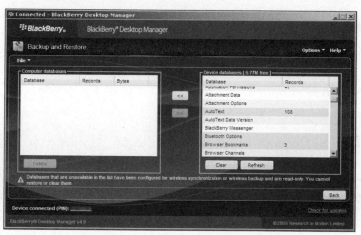

Figure 16-6:
The advanced Backup and Restore screen.

3. **In the left list, Ctrl+click the databases you want to back up.**

4. **Click the left-facing (backup) arrow.**

   A progress bar moves while your BlackBerry Storm is backed up. This step merely transfers the databases onto your PC; it doesn't save them. When the backup transfer is finished, you can see the two databases on the left side of the window.

5. **Choose File⇨Save As.**

   A file chooser appears.

6. **Name your file and specify where you want to save it on your PC.**

   This saves your selective backup on your PC. Make sure to name it something specific so you know what exactly is in the backup.

Looking at backup BlackBerry files

Whether you use the one button-push backup method or you manually back up your file, the file is saved on your PC as an `.ipd` file. Those curious readers out there might be asking, "Can I read these backup files without a BlackBerry?" The answer is yes! With a third-party product called ABC Amber BlackBerry Converter, you can view any `.ipd` file. What's the point? Suppose you lost your BlackBerry Storm but need to read an old e-mail or to get contacts from your backup files. This tool allows you to convert anything in your backup file (e-mails, SMS messages, PIM messages, and contacts) into PDF or Word documents. For more information and to try ABC Amber BlackBerry Converter for free, go to `www.processtext.com/abcblackberry.html`.

Because anyone with Amber BlackBerry Converter can look into your backups, make sure you secure your backup files so only you can get to it.

You need to manually save the backup file on your PC even after you choose a location for the file in Step 3. A selective backup doesn't automatically save your backup on your PC.

Restoring, your way

However, when restoring selectively, you must already have a backup file to restore from. Although this might sound obvious, the point we're making is that you can selectively restore from any backup — auto or manual.

For example, say you have autobackup running every other day, and you want to restore only your e-mail messages from two days ago. You don't need to do a full restore; that would overwrite the new contact you put in your Contacts yesterday. Rather, you can use the selective restore method and get back only your e-mail messages.

To restore your way, follow these steps:

1. **From the BDM, double-click the Backup and Restore icon.**

   The Backup and Restore screen appears.

2. **Click the Advanced button.**

   The advanced Backup and Restore screen appears; refer to Figure 16-6. The right side of the screen shows your different information categories, or *databases*.

3. **Choose File⇨Open.**

   A window opens so you can choose which backup file you want to restore from.

   A BlackBerry backup file has an `.ipd` extension.

4. **Select a backup file.**

5. **Click the Open button.**

   The different information categories, or databases, appear on the left side of the screen. You're now ready for a selective restore.

6. **Select categories (or databases).**

   You can select multiple databases by Ctrl+clicking the databases you want.

7. **Click the right-facing (Restore) arrow.**

   You'll likely see a warning window asking whether you want to replace all the information with the data you're restoring. Refer to Figure 16-5.

   If your BlackBerry Storm has the same categories as the ones you're restoring (which is likely), you'll overwrite *any* information you have on your BlackBerry.

   You can confidently move on to Step 8 if you know the database you're restoring has the information you're looking for.

8. **Click OK.**

   A progress bar appears while the selective restore is going. When the progress bar window disappears, the information categories that you've selected are restored on your BlackBerry.

Clearing BlackBerry information, your way

You can also delete information on your BlackBerry Storm from BlackBerry Desktop Manager. When would you use *selective deletion?*

Suppose you want to clear only your phone logs from your BlackBerry. One way is to tediously select one phone log at a time and press Delete, repeating until all phone logs are gone. However, you could delete a database from the advanced Backup and Restore screen by using the Backup and Restore function.

To selectively delete databases on your BlackBerry, follow these steps:

1. **From BDM on your PC, double-click the Backup and Restore icon.**

   The Backup and Restore screen appears.

2. **Click the Advanced button.**

   The advanced Backup and Restore screen appears; refer to Figure 16-6. The right side of the screen shows your BlackBerry's different databases.

3. **Ctrl+click the database(s) you want to delete.**

   The database is highlighted.

4. **Click the Clear button on the right side of the screen.**

   A warning window asks you to confirm your deletion.

5. **Click OK.**

   A progress bar shows the deletion. When the progress bar disappears, the information categories you selected are cleared from your BlackBerry.

Backing Up and Restoring Wirelessly

Yes, that is right! Your BlackBerry Storm can do this without being on BES. However, you do have to pay a little bit for this service; at the time of writing, they're in private beta.

The product is SmrtGuard, www.SmrtGuard.com. *SmrtGuard* is a piece of software that sits on your Storm that can wirelessly back up your data. Currently, SmrtGuard supports address book contacts, memos, and to-dos and is planning to support calendars, pictures, and phone logs in the near future.

In addition to its backup and restore capabilities, SmrtGuard also has features to help you locate, recover, and destroy device-side data. SmrtGuard has a tracking or *lojack* feature that helps you determine whether you simply misplaced your device or whether your device is stolen. After you determine that your device is stolen, you can send a signal to have your data destroyed via the SmrtGuard Dashboard on www.SmrtGuard.com.

We'll have more information as SmrtGuard cooks up more features. Be sure to check our Web site at www.BlackBerryForDummies.com and check www.SmrtGuard.com for more on this.

Chapter 17

Installing and Managing Third-Party Applications

. . . .

In This Chapter

▶ Getting started with Application Loader

▶ Installing a BlackBerry application

▶ Uninstalling an application

▶ Upgrading your operating system

▶ Browsing and installing AppCenter and StoreFront

. . . .

*I*n this book's Parts of Tens, we point out a few great applications that make your BlackBerry that much more productive. We also reveal a few games that make your BlackBerry more entertaining than ever.

Think of your BlackBerry as a mini laptop where you can run preinstalled applications as well as install new applications. You can even upgrade your BlackBerry's operating system. (Yup, that's right; your BlackBerry even has an operating system.)

We start this chapter by introducing Application Loader, which allows you to load applications (who'd have guessed?) onto your BlackBerry. Then we show you how to install and uninstall an application from your BlackBerry. Finally, we show you how to use Application Loader to upgrade your operating system.

Accessing Application Loader

In this chapter, as with other chapters in Part IV, you work closely with your PC and your BlackBerry Storm. On your PC, you use an application called BlackBerry Desktop Manager (BDM), which comes on a CD along with your BlackBerry. For an introduction to BlackBerry Desktop Manager, see Chapter 14. Application Loader is in BlackBerry Desktop Manager.

After installing BlackBerry Desktop Manager on your PC, do the following to access Application Loader:

1. **On your PC, select Start⇨Programs⇨BlackBerry⇨Desktop Manager.**

   BlackBerry Desktop Manager opens.

2. **Connect your BlackBerry Storm to your PC via your USB cable.**

   Doing so connects your Storm to your PC. If successful, you see the password dialog box, as shown in Figure 17-1. If not, see whether the USB cable is connected properly to both your PC and your Storm and then try again. If all else fails, contact the technical support of your service provider.

Figure 17-1:
The password dialog box on your PC.

> **Device Password Required**
>
> Device: USB-PIN: 247134F9
> Please enter your device password (1/10).
>
> Password: [   ]
>
> [OK]   [Cancel]

3. **Enter your password.**

   Your BlackBerry Storm-to-PC connection is complete.

4. **On your PC, double-click the Application Loader icon in BlackBerry Desktop Manager.**

   The Application Loader screen opens, as shown in Figure 17-2. At this point, you're ready to use the Application Loader.

Figure 17-2:
The Application Loader screen.

Installing an Application

In this chapter, we install iSkoot for Skype for BlackBerry. *iSkoot* is a free application that connects to the Web directly and allows you to use Skype. You can download this application at `www.download.com/iSkoot-for-Skype-BlackBerry-/3000-7242_4-10797721.html`.

No matter what application you're installing from your PC to your BlackBerry Storm, the steps are the same. As of this writing, vendors haven't published updated versions of their products that support Storm. But you can use the following steps as a guide to installing the application of your choice.

1. **Install the application on your PC.**

   The installation onto your PC varies, depending on the application, so refer to its manual.

2. **Locate the application's ALX file.**

   You can usually find a file with the `.alx` extension in the folder where you installed the application on your PC.

   The ALX file doesn't get installed on your Storm; rather, it tells Application Loader where the actual application file is located on your PC.

3. **Click Application Loader from BlackBerry Desktop Manager.**

   The Application Loader screen shows. Refer to Figure 17-2.

4. **Click the Start button below Add/Remove Applications.**

   The screen listing of what applications to install appears.

5. **Click the Browse button and locate and select the ALX file you want to install.**

   The ALX file is usually in the folder where you installed the application on your PC.

   You return to the Application Loader screen, where iSkoot is one of the applications in the list, as shown in Figure 17-3.

6. **Select iSkoot Skype for Blackberry and click Next.**

   A summary screen shows up listing only the applications that will be installed or upgraded.

7. **Click Finish.**

   The installation process starts, and a progress window appears. When the progress window disappears — and if all went well — the application is on your BlackBerry Storm. The application should be under the Applications folder of your BlackBerry Storm.

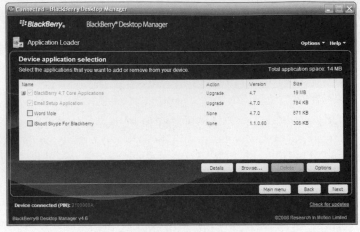

Figure 17-3:
Your appli-
cation is
added to
the list of
installed
and can be
installed
into Storm.

If you get an invalid signature error after clicking the Finish button:

- ✔ **You didn't get your Storm from your employer:** Something is probably wrong with the application. You need to contact the software vendor.

- ✔ **You got your BlackBerry from your employer:** You don't have permission to install applications on your BlackBerry. The IT department rules the school.

You don't have to use Application Loader to get the goods onto your BlackBerry. You can install applications other ways as well:

- ✔ Wirelessly through an *over-the-air (OTA)* download. See Chapter 9 for more on wireless installations.

- ✔ BlackBerry Enterprise Server (BES) wireless install (if your BlackBerry is employer provided). In this case, you have no control over the installation process. Your company's BlackBerry system administrator controls which applications are on your BlackBerry.

Uninstalling an Application

You can uninstall an application in two ways:

- ✔ Using Application Loader
- ✔ Using your BlackBerry handheld

As in the preceding section on installing, we use iSkoot as an example and assume that you already installed the iSkoot application. Of course, you can follow the same steps for uninstalling other applications.

Uninstalling with Application Loader

The steps to uninstalling a BlackBerry application are similar to installing:

1. **On your PC, launch Application Loader.**

2. **Click Next.**

3. **Enter your password; refer to Figure 17-1.**

   If your handheld isn't connected properly, the PIN of your device won't show up in the Application Loader screen. Refer to Figure 17-2. Connect your Storm to the USB cable and connect the USB cable to the PC.

   After entering your password, the Application Loader screen indicates that your device is connected.

4. **Click the Start button below Add/Remove Applications.**

   The screen listing of applications appears similar to Figure 17-3.

5. **Scroll to the application you want to delete and clear its check box.**

   The Action column for iSkoot indicates Remove.

6. **Click Next.**

   A Summary screen listing the action of the Application Loader shows up. It lists iSkoot to be removed from your BlackBerry.

7. **Click Finish.**

   The uninstall process starts, and a progress window appears. When the progress window disappears, you have uninstalled the application from your Storm.

Uninstalling with your BlackBerry handheld

When you don't have access to your PC, you can uninstall an application from your BlackBerry handheld:

1. **Touch-press the Options icon from the BlackBerry Home screen.**

   The Options application opens. If you're holding Storm in portrait mode, press the menu key to find the Options icon.

2. **Scroll to Advanced Options and select Applications.**

   The list of applications installed on your Storm appears, as shown in Figure 17-4.

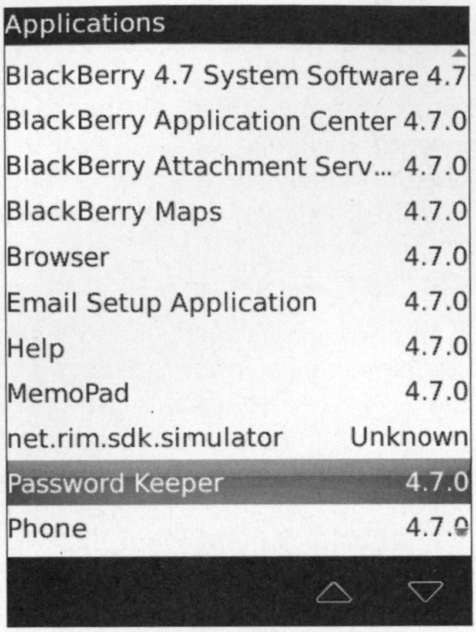

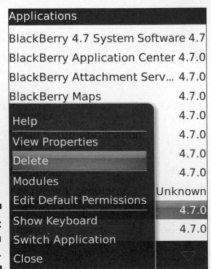

Figure 17-4:
The list of
applications
installed in
your Storm.

3. **Scroll to the application you want to delete and press the menu key.**

4. **Touch-press Delete (see Figure 17-5).**

   A confirmation dialog box appears.

5. **Touch-press Delete to confirm the deletion.**

   You're given a choice to restart now or at a later time. After restarting, the deleted application is uninstalled.

Figure 17-5:
Deleting an
application.

Upgrading Your BlackBerry OS

Your Storm is RIM's latest product as of this writing and should come with the latest version of BlackBerry *operating system (OS)*. So, you shouldn't need this section for some time. But when it comes down to it, the BlackBerry OS update comes from BlackBerry Handheld Software, which is available from two sources:

- ✔ Your network service provider
- ✔ Your BlackBerry system administrator

The handheld software may differ from provider to provider, so get it from the service provider's Web site. We compiled a location of the download pages for different service providers at www.blackberryfordummies.com/bhs.html.

In this section, we assume that the latest BlackBerry Handheld Software for Storm is already installed on your PC. For help with installing BlackBerry Handheld Software, refer to the instructions that come with it.

You should upgrade your BlackBerry OS only when you have to or are told to by your network service provider or your corporate BlackBerry system administrator. We discourage you from upgrading; why ruin a good thing? The risk of losing data is always there — as well as the risk that things that won't work as well as before.

To address the risk of information loss, RIM designed Application Loader to automatically back up for you as part of the OS upgrade. However, our experience has taught us to perform a full backup manually as an extra precaution. The Application Loader backup isn't always complete in our experience. See Chapter 16 for more on backing up data manually.

After you finish a manual backup of your BlackBerry Storm, you can start the upgrade process by doing the following:

1. **Enter your BlackBerry Storm password (if you had set one) into BlackBerry Desktop Manager on your PC.**

2. **Click Application Loader on the Desktop Manager screen.**

   The Application Loader screen appears, as shown earlier in Figure 17-2.

3. **Click the Start button below Add/Remove Applications.**

   A list of software appears, as shown in Figure 17-6.

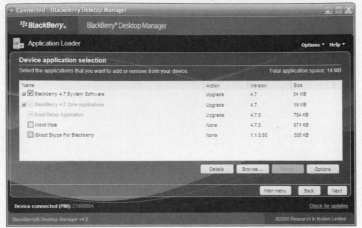

Figure 17-6:
Application
updates
that are
available.

4. **With your mouse, you can opt out of the upgrade by deselecting the OS portion.**

This appears as BlackBerry 4.7 System Software in Figure 17-6.

The OS is listed only if you need an upgrade — it means that your BlackBerry OS is out of date. If the OS doesn't appear in the list, the handheld software you installed on the desktop machine is the same as the one installed on your device, or a prior version compared to the one installed on your device.

You also need to back up your device in case something goes wrong on the upgrade. Backup options can be done through the Options button.

5. **Click the Options button.**

The Options screen appears, as shown in Figure 17-7. This is where you decide whether you want to back up your BlackBerry content before upgrading your OS.

We recommend selecting Back Up Device Automatically During the Installation Process.

Figure 17-7:
Command
Application
Loader to
back up the
device here
(Options
screen).

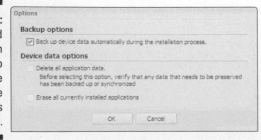

6. **Select Backup and click OK.**

   You're back on the previous screen as shown in Figure 17-6.

7. **Click the Next button.**

   A summary page confirms your actions. A final chance for you to either proceed with the OS upgrade or not.

8. **Click the Finish button.**

   The BlackBerry OS upgrade starts, complete with a progress window showing a series of steps and a progress bar. The entire process takes ten minutes or more, depending on your PC model and the OS version you're upgrading to.

   At times during the BlackBerry OS upgrade, your BlackBerry Storm display goes on and off. Don't worry; this is normal.

   When the progress window disappears, the OS upgrade is complete.

Finding and Installing Applications from App Stores

With the success of iPhone App Store, several copycats are sprouting everywhere for other platforms including the BlackBerry. App Store is an application that behaves as storefronts showcasing applications that you can download directly to your device. Applications can be either free or needs your credit card number:

- ✔ **Handango (www.handango.com):** Handango is one of the oldest storefronts selling applications for the mobile devices. The company started selling apps through the Web but now have an app store that you can download from the Web site.

- ✔ **CrackBerry On-Device App Store (http://CrackBerryAppStore.com):** Partnering with Mobihand, CrackBerry also provides an app store where you can find great applications to download.

- ✔ **BlackBerry Application Center:** This app store is still cooking in RIM's oven as of this writing but the concept is the same. Check our companion Web site (www.blackberryfordummies.com) regularly for updates. We'll post a download link when it becomes available.

Part V
The Part of Tens

The 5th Wave   By Rich Tennant

Mitch would never be sure it was laughter he heard that day at the airport, but he never again traveled with his Pez PDA.

In this part . . .

If the earlier parts of this book are the cake and frosting, this part is the cherry on top. Delve into these three short but sweet chapters to find BlackBerry accessories, applications to max your BlackBerry experience, and ten Websites to check out on your BlackBerry. And remember that you can always visit us for an up-to-date The Part of Tens at www.BlackBerryForDummies.com.

Chapter 18

Ten Great BlackBerry Storm Accessories

The BlackBerry retail box contains a few essentials: a battery, a charger, a micro USB cable, and a belt clip. If you're like us, though, you're not satisfied with what is included in the box. In this chapter we present the accessories that we think supplement your BlackBerry well — and we tell you where to shop for them.

Please check our companion Web site, www.blackberryfordummies.com, for an updated accessories list.

microSD Card

Your new BlackBerry Storm may or may not come with external memory: a *microSD card.* And we bet that is the first thing you'll be looking for after you get your BlackBerry Storm. After all, you want to carry with you a boatload of music and video files, right? Many electronic gadgets use microSD cards, so they're easy to find.

A normal price range at the time of this writing is $20 for a 4GB capacity and $30 for an 8GB capacity. Your best bet of finding a good deal is on the Internet. Special promotions come and go, but we noticed that there's always a good deal somewhere. Our best advice is to just shop around. And for any Internet purchase, take into consideration the shipping and handling costs plus the vendor's return policy (or lack thereof).

Any brand will do, as long as you make sure you're buying a microSD card.

BlackBerry Remote Stereo Gateway

Do you want to make your home-entertainment center play the music in your BlackBerry Storm? The Remote Stereo Gateway is for you. Connect this tiny device to your stereo system and you can transmit music wirelessly from your BlackBerry Storm (for about $90).

You can get it from RIM's shopping site at www.shopblackberry.com.

Stereo Headsets

Although your new BlackBerry is a stereo music player, it doesn't come with stereo headphones. You will definitely yearn for stereo sound the moment you listen to music or watch video clips. A quick search on the Internet for BlackBerry Storm + stereo headphones yields many results. But you want to be able to talk too.

You could spend $30 to $200. We like several:

- ✔ BlackBerry stereo headset with noise-isolating ear gels
- ✔ V-MODA Vibe duo in-ear headphones with mic
- ✔ Motorola S9 stereo Bluetooth headset

The best place to get stereo headphones for your BlackBerry is good ol' Amazon: www.amazon.com.

Case and Belt Clip

You have plenty of cases to choose from, with looks ranging from sporty to professional. These cases will set you back anywhere from $20 to $40, which isn't too bad for looking hip.

Here's where you can buy a new case or belt clip:

✔ crackberry.com
✔ www.bberry.com
✔ www.blackberryden.com
✔ www.blackberrysource.com
✔ www.blackberrystuff.com

When you buy a new belt case or clip, buy one made specifically for BlackBerry Storm.

Screen Protector

If the protector case described in the preceding section is a bit stressful for your wallet, try Blackberry Storm Pro high-definition screen protector with mirror effect. That's a mouthful, but for about $10 it protects your screen from scratches. Go to accessorygeeks.com.

Extra Battery

An extra battery for your BlackBerry Storm will come in handy if you're a daily user. We recommend buying your battery only from Research In Motion at www.shopblackberry.com, and not from some other manufacturer. A faulty battery can damage your BlackBerry beyond repair.

Make sure the battery you buy is for your BlackBerry model. You'll spend around $50 for the extra battery.

Battery Charger

If you watch video on your BlackBerry Storm, you know the battery needs to be charged every couple of hours. And if you're always on the go, you better have a portable charger on hand. The charger included with your BlackBerry is great to carry around town (and the world) because it has multiple adapters for different countries' electric plugs.

If you're a road warrior, we recommend the BlackBerry car charger. It will set you back around $30.

Make sure that the charger you buy is for your BlackBerry model.

You can get a BlackBerry car charger from the following:

- ✔ shop.crackberry.com
- ✔ www.blackberrysource.com
- ✔ www.blackberrystuff.com
- ✔ shopblackberry.com (RIM's official store)

Full Keyboard

If you write long e-mails or draft long proposals on your BlackBerry Storm, a full-sized keyboard is perfect for you. You'll save time and your thumbs.

You have your choice of Bluetooth and non-Bluetooth connection options. We recommend Bluetooth to minimize the clutter. A Bluetooth keyboard is the most convenient option for the obvious reasons: You don't have to carry cables, and you can position your BlackBerry any way you want.

For less than $100, you can own the cool iGo Stowaway Ultra-Slim Bluetooth keyboard, available at www.amazon.com. Or you can buy the ThinkOutside Stowaway Shasta Bluetooth keyboard for BlackBerry, available at yahooshopping.com for $45.

External Speaker

BlackBerry comes with a speaker, but if the sound quality just isn't good enough for your listening taste, an external Bluetooth speaker can bring your outdoor listening to the next level:

- ✔ Blueant M1 Bluetooth stereo speakers
- ✔ Motorola EQ5 wireless travel stereo speaker

For about $110, you can get either of them from `shop.crackberry.com`.

Car Mount

To complete your BlackBerry car experience, mount your BlackBerry in your car. The market offers many products ranging from $15 to $30. You can search from major sites. You can get also get it from BlackBerry sites:

- ✔ `shop.crackberry.com`
- ✔ `www.blackberrysource.com`
- ✔ `www.blackberrystuff.com`

Make sure the product you're picking supports BlackBerry Storm.

Chapter 19

Ten Must-Have BlackBerry Programs

*T*he industry of BlackBerry software is growing at a dizzying rate. At the time we're writing this book, many software vendors have said they will support Storm but haven't yet rolled out a Storm version. But we are almost certain with the BlackBerry world taken by Storm, the software titles will blow you away.

These choices are the results of finding out what people use via either message board posts or commentaries in the public domain. The applications featured here are just the tip of the iceberg. By all means, surf the Internet; more software will be available by the time you're reading this.

And don't forget to visit our Web site for updates at www.blackberry fordummies.com.

PeeKaWho: E-Mail and SMS Preview

Have you ever wished that your BlackBerry had an e-mail notifier? You know, the kind you're used to in Outlook or Google Notifier? Say you're typing an e-mail reply to set up a meeting time and place, but suddenly your BlackBerry vibrates, which means a new e-mail just arrived. You want to check that new e-mail, so you first save your e-mail as draft and then go back to the inbox and open the e-mail to read. Ahh, painful.

Imagine you have PeeKaWho. Now when you get a new e-mail, you immediately see who sent it, and you get a message preview. Simple, to the point, and we love it. Don't take our word for it; try PeeKaWho at `smrtguard.com/peek.jsp`.

Slacker

If you like streaming music, you'll like Slacker on the BlackBerry Storm. You can search through the online selection of songs and personalize a playlist. If you've used Pandora music service on your desktop, you're familiar. The application can also store music on your BlackBerry microSD card so you can listen offline. For more information, go to `www.Slacker.com`.

BerryStore

Your BlackBerry Storm comes with the Application Center where you can directly download applications. Most of those applications have been filtered by the network carriers, which most of the time is a good thing; they make sure the software in the Application Center is compatible with your BlackBerry Storm.

However, if you want to find some gems, we recommend downloading BerryStore, which works similar to Application Center. Download applications from it and find cool new applications to try. Download BerryStore at `www.berrystore.com`.

SmrtGuard: Your BlackBerry Guardian

What would happen to your data if you lost your BlackBerry? Sensitive e-mails, your phone call histories, your contacts, and all your appointments? It's scary to think of a stranger getting to know you this way.

Thankfully there's SmrtGuard (formerly known as BerryFinder.com), which provides the following tools:

- ✓ **Locate and track your BlackBerry:** You can track (without a GPS) whether your BlackBerry is being taken or see its approximate location. Did you simply misplace your BlackBerry or did someone actually steal it?

- ✓ **Wireless data backup:** This is another must-have feature that SmrtGuard provides. If you actually self-destroyed your data and don't have a backup, the scheduled wireless backup of your PIM (calendar, memo, tasks) data comes in handy. From its Web site, you can even see and browse through your backed-up data and export to a file (Excel or text).

- ✓ **Sounding the homing beacon:** If you simply misplaced your BlackBerry but can't find it by calling (you muted it), no worries. Just send a homing beacon, and your BlackBerry emits a loud sound regardless of your profile setting. We wish our remote controls had this feature!

- ✓ **Self-destruct in five seconds:** Okay, not in five seconds, but you can decide when to destroy all your BlackBerry data. That includes e-mails, contacts, appointments, to-dos, memos, phone logs, and all the files on your microSD.

Always protect your BlackBerry with a password. That way your data will erase after ten unsuccessful password entries. However, it doesn't delete the files on your microSD. This is why SmrtGuard is so helpful.

With a BlackBerry guardian by your side, you can worry about your business instead of your BlackBerry data being stolen. Register your BlackBerry at www.SmrtGuard.com.

Handmark Pocket Express

If we have to recommend one application, Pocket Express is it. This handy, reliable tool gets news and other information such as weather, sports updates, maps, and stocks. The user interface is intuitive, and you can buy other applications from Pocket Express. And the best part? It's almost free. (Pocket Express charges a fee for accessing premium channels.) Download Pocket Express from your BlackBerry at express.handmark.com.

Google Talk Mobile and Yahoo! Messenger Mobile

If you currently use Google Talk or Yahoo! Messenger on your PC, try the mobile version. To download, point your BlackBerry browser to one of these URLs:

- Google Talk Mobile at `www.blackberry.com/GoogleTalk`
- Yahoo! Messenger Mobile at `www.blackberry.com/YahooDownload`

iSkoot Skype Client

Are you a big Skype fan? Now you don't have to sit on your computer to use the service. The folks at iSkoot make it possible to fully use Skype functionality from your BlackBerry. Calling a Skype buddy? No problem. Chatting with your Skype friends? That's what this program is for. Plus, it's free! To download it from your PC, go to `www.iskoot.com`.

MobiTV

TV on your BlackBerry? That's right. MobiTV streams live television to your BlackBerry for a fee. You can find channels like CNBC, Discovery Channel, and a whole lot more. At the time of this writing, MobiTV only supports BlackBerry 8130 (the Pearl). But check on its Web site for a version on the BlackBerry Storm. To get started, go to `www.mobitv.com/gettv/`.

Bookworm

A warning: The Bookworm word game is addictive. It is part crossword puzzle, part word jumble, and part arcade puzzler. Your job is to feed Lex, the hungry bookworm, with words. You can buy it or download a free trial version at `bb.magmic.com/game?show=Bookworm`.

Chuzzle

Chuzzle is a game similar to Tetris and KaGlom (another fun BlackBerry game). Chuzzle is a furry little ball that, when you match three of the same color, explodes. This game is quite engaging and full of good fun. Try it out at hbplay.com/item/Chuzzle.

Chapter 20

Ten Web Site Categories for Storm Browsing

*W*eb surfing with a BlackBerry has improved dramatically with the newer models. With higher screen resolution and bigger real estate, your Storm should give you one of the best mobile Web-browsing experiences. Prior to Storm, we would tell you where to find Web sites designed for mobile devices because most Web pages displayed horribly on the older devices. That's not the case anymore; most Web pages now display just as good in Storm. So, the browsing habit you have on your PC can now be maintained in Storm.

These Web site recommendations are based on reviews in the public domain and sites that definitely help you on the go.

Weather

Weather changes quite often, but you can keep up with the sites in this section.

- ✓ **AccuWeather.com (`www.accuweather.com`):** AccuWeather.com provides the local weather forecast.

- ✓ **Weather.com (`www.weather.com`):** Weather.com is smart enough to know that you're using a mobile device and displays a nice trim version of its page with few links to non-weather–related information.

If these two sites aren't good enough, check out the "Portals" section later in this chapter. Major portals have weather information as well as traffic alerts and airport delays.

News

Most major news companies have mobile versions of their sites. This section is just a sampling of what's out there. We list the same Web address as you would expect when browsing from your desktop. These sites detect that you're using a SmartPhone and redirect you to the mobile-friendly version of their sites:

- ✓ **ABC News (`www.abcnews.com`):** Get ABC News on TV on your BlackBerry.

- ✓ **BBC News (`www.bbc.com`):** You can read the BBC News right from your BlackBerry Storm, even if you're not in the UK.

- ✓ **CNN (`cnn.com`):** This is CNN's mobile-friendly Web site.

- ✓ **The New York Times (`www.nytimes.com`):** This automatically points to the *New York Times* mobile-friendly Web site, a clean and easy site to navigate without a lot of advertisements.

- ✓ **Reuters (`www.reuters.com`):** A mobile-friendly version of the Reuters site.

- ✓ **USA Today (`usatoday.com`):** *USA Today,* one of the most popular newspapers, is now available for free from your BlackBerry.

- ✓ **Wired News (`mobile.wired.com`):** Wired News is the mobile version of this tech news Web site.

Searches, Directories, and Portals

The sites in this section are *Web portals,* which are sites that contain various information or links to other sites.

- ✔ **Google** (www.google.com): The king of search engines works like a charm in your Storm.

- ✔ **MSN** (msn.com): You can access MSN Hotmail, MSN Messenger, and an online calendar. It has all the features that you can find in a Web portal, such as Web search, weather lookup, sports information, and news. Plus you get their finance-related pages, which give you up-to-the-minute stock quotes.

- ✔ **RIM mobile home page** (mobile.blackberry.com): This is the default home page setting for most BlackBerry browsers. The service provider can customize it, though, so your BlackBerry browser may point to your service provider's home page. RIM's home page is definitely a place to start browsing the Web.

  You should definitely bookmark this site.

- ✔ **Yahoo! Mobile** (www.yahoo.com): Yahoo! is a smart portal because it knows you're using a mobile device and formats the page accordingly, meaning a smaller page with no advertisements. The portal site allows BlackBerry users to employ regular Yahoo! functions, such as Yahoo! Mail, Messenger, Finance, and Games, as well as driving directions and weather.

  You should definitely bookmark this site.

Business

You can keep up with the latest news of the finance world from your BlackBerry. Visit the sites in this section for finance-related articles and news.

- ✔ **BusinessWeek Online** (www.businessweek.com): This is another place to get great finance information.

- ✔ **Fidelity** (fidelity.com): Fidelity is an online investment brokerage firm.

- ✔ **Yahoo! Finance** (finance.yahoo.com): This is a great site for checking your stock information.

Travel

Every site in Table 20-1 features flight status and gate numbers. Some allow you to log on (if you're part of their frequent-flier program) to access frequent-flier benefits.

Table 20-1	BlackBerry-Accessible Travel Sites
Airline	*Mobile Web Site*
Air Canada	`aircanada.ca`
American Airlines	`aa.flightlookup.com/omnisky`
British Airways	`www.britishairways.com`
Cathay Pacific	`cathaypacific.com`
Continental Airlines	`continental.com`
Delta	`delta.com`
JetBlue	`jetblue.com`
Northwest Airlines	`nwa.com`
United Air Lines	`ua2go.com`
Any airline	`flightview.com`

- ✔ **TripKick (`www.tripkick.com`):** Don't be so excited about getting a good deal on a hotel only to end up in a crummy room. TripKick tells you who has the best rooms and who doesn't.

- ✔ **WikiTravel (`www.wikitravel.com`):** One of the most up-to-date and complete travel guides on the Web.

Sports

Missing updates on your favorite sport while on the go? You don't have to. Visit any of the sports-related sites in this section, and you'll get the scoop on what's happening to your favorite team.

- ✔ **CBS SportsLine.com (`sportsline.com/mobile`):** If you're active on CBS Fantasy Team, you'll be happy to know you can log in and view your stats from this Web site. Popular U.S. sports are covered here.

- ✔ **ESPN (`mobileapp.espn.go.com`):** Everyone knows ESPN. This is the mobile version of its Web site.

Advice and Self Help

For those of you who frequent Home Depot, this section could be a big time-saver.

- ✔ **HowCast** (`www.howcast.com`): With a dose of humor, this site is a world of how-to videos.

- ✔ **Omiru** (`www.omiru.com`): This site offers practical fashion advice for the common person.

- ✔ **Yahoo! Answer** (`answers.yahoo.com`): Here you can get all sorts of creative, amusing, and helpful responses to your questions — advice that's free.

- ✔ **Zeer** (`www.zeer.com`): No need to stand in the supermarket comparing nutritional labels; do it here.

Social and Virtual Networking

For those of you who are (or aren't yet) addicted to social networking sites, we list the popular ones here. There are so many of these that if your favorite site is not listed here, don't fret, just type the address in your Storm Browser.

- ✔ **Facebook** (`www.facebook.com`): In a general category, which is open to 13 and older, the site attracts the after-college crowd.

- ✔ **Friendster** (`www.friendster.com`): Popular in Southeast Asian countries and open to people 16 and older.

- ✔ **Multiply** (`www.multiply.com`): Claims to focus on real-world relationships and open to 13 and older. It's a popular site for teenagers.

- ✔ **MySpace** (`myspace.com`): Also in the general public category. It is open to 14 and older and attracts high school and college kids.

- ✔ **Linked-In** (`linkedin.com`): Catering to professional and business relationships. You'll find people publishing their bios on their profile.

Shopping and Shipping Information

Shopaholics can keep it up online even when they're not in front of the PC.

- ✔ **Amazon** (`www.amazon.com`): With Amazon Anywhere, you can shop and check your account information right from your BlackBerry.

- **eBay (`www.ebay.com`):** You can bid as a buyer right from the convenience of your BlackBerry Storm.

- **FedEx tracking (`www.fedex.com`):** This mobile version of the FedEx Web site allows you to track packages right from your BlackBerry.

- **Gas Buddy (`www.gasbuddy.com`):** You can find the nearest gas station selling the cheapest gas.

- **ILikeTotallyLoveIt.com (`www.iliketotallyloveit.com`):** Shopping with a twist. Shoppers post things they like. Pretty much anything, from wasabi gumballs to Delorean cars, and solicit opinions on posted sale items from other members.

- **UPS tracking (`www.ups.com`):** Like FedEx, UPS also has a mobile version of its Web site that allows you to track packages right from your BlackBerry.

Other Browsing Categories

You can visit the following sites from your BlackBerry to get more information on various topics.

- **BlackBerryGoodies (`blackberrygoodies.com`):** Go here from your BlackBerry Storm or from your PC. You can get information on customizing your BlackBerry Storm, read Storm application reviews, and get answers to your Storm-related questions — from us!

- **MiniSphere (`www.minisphere.com`):** You find useful links designed for mobile devices here.

- **wcities (`pda.wcities.com`):** The wcities site provides searches based on the city you select. You can search city information, dining, shopping, and sport and local events.

- **Starbucks Locator (`starbucks.com`):** This site helps you locate the nearest Starbucks so you can meet your buddies or get a dose of caffeine.

- **MizPee (`mizpee.com`):** When you have to go, you have to go. This site locates the nearest bathroom.

Index

• F •

• G •

BUSINESS, CAREERS & PERSONAL FINANCE

Accounting For Dummies, 4th Edition*
978-0-470-24600-9

Bookkeeping Workbook For Dummies†
978-0-470-16983-4

Commodities For Dummies
978-0-470-04928-0

Doing Business in China For Dummies
978-0-470-04929-7

E-Mail Marketing For Dummies
978-0-470-19087-6

Job Interviews For Dummies, 3rd Edition*†
978-0-470-17748-8

Personal Finance Workbook For Dummies*†
978-0-470-09933-9

Real Estate License Exams For Dummies
978-0-7645-7623-2

Six Sigma For Dummies
978-0-7645-6798-8

Small Business Kit For Dummies, 2nd Edition*†
978-0-7645-5984-6

Telephone Sales For Dummies
978-0-470-16836-3

BUSINESS PRODUCTIVITY & MICROSOFT OFFICE

Access 2007 For Dummies
978-0-470-03649-5

Excel 2007 For Dummies
978-0-470-03737-9

Office 2007 For Dummies
978-0-470-00923-9

Outlook 2007 For Dummies
978-0-470-03830-7

PowerPoint 2007 For Dummies
978-0-470-04059-1

Project 2007 For Dummies
978-0-470-03651-8

QuickBooks 2008 For Dummies
978-0-470-18470-7

Quicken 2008 For Dummies
978-0-470-17473-9

Salesforce.com For Dummies, 2nd Edition
978-0-470-04893-1

Word 2007 For Dummies
978-0-470-03658-7

EDUCATION, HISTORY, REFERENCE & TEST PREPARATION

African American History For Dummies
978-0-7645-5469-8

Algebra For Dummies
978-0-7645-5325-7

Algebra Workbook For Dummies
978-0-7645-8467-1

Art History For Dummies
978-0-470-09910-0

ASVAB For Dummies, 2nd Edition
978-0-470-10671-6

British Military History For Dummies
978-0-470-03213-8

Calculus For Dummies
978-0-7645-2498-1

Canadian History For Dummies, 2nd Edition
978-0-470-83656-9

Geometry Workbook For Dummies
978-0-471-79940-5

The SAT I For Dummies, 6th Edition
978-0-7645-7193-0

Series 7 Exam For Dummies
978-0-470-09932-2

World History For Dummies
978-0-7645-5242-7

FOOD, GARDEN, HOBBIES & HOME

Bridge For Dummies, 2nd Edition
978-0-471-92426-5

Coin Collecting For Dummies, 2nd Edition
978-0-470-22275-1

Cooking Basics For Dummies, 3rd Edition
978-0-7645-7206-7

Drawing For Dummies
978-0-7645-5476-6

Etiquette For Dummies, 2nd Edition
978-0-470-10672-3

Gardening Basics For Dummies*†
978-0-470-03749-2

Knitting Patterns For Dummies
978-0-470-04556-5

Living Gluten-Free For Dummies†
978-0-471-77383-2

Painting Do-It-Yourself For Dummies
978-0-470-17533-0

HEALTH, SELF HELP, PARENTING & PETS

Anger Management For Dummies
978-0-470-03715-7

Anxiety & Depression Workbook For Dummies
978-0-7645-9793-0

Dieting For Dummies, 2nd Edition
978-0-7645-4149-0

Dog Training For Dummies, 2nd Edition
978-0-7645-8418-3

Horseback Riding For Dummies
978-0-470-09719-9

Infertility For Dummies†
978-0-470-11518-3

Meditation For Dummies with CD-ROM, 2nd Edition
978-0-471-77774-8

Post-Traumatic Stress Disorder For Dummies
978-0-470-04922-8

Puppies For Dummies, 2nd Edition
978-0-470-03717-1

Thyroid For Dummies, 2nd Edition†
978-0-471-78755-6

Type 1 Diabetes For Dummies*†
978-0-470-17811-9

INTERNET & DIGITAL MEDIA

AdWords For Dummies
978-0-470-15252-2

Blogging For Dummies, 2nd Edition
978-0-470-23017-6

Digital Photography All-in-One Desk Reference For Dummies, 3rd Edition
978-0-470-03743-0

Digital Photography For Dummies, 5th Edition
978-0-7645-9802-9

Digital SLR Cameras & Photography For Dummies, 2nd Edition
978-0-470-14927-0

eBay Business All-in-One Desk Reference For Dummies
978-0-7645-8438-1

eBay For Dummies, 5th Edition*
978-0-470-04529-9

eBay Listings That Sell For Dummies
978-0-471-78912-3

Facebook For Dummies
978-0-470-26273-3

The Internet For Dummies, 11th Edition
978-0-470-12174-0

Investing Online For Dummies, 5th Edition
978-0-7645-8456-5

iPod & iTunes For Dummies, 5th Editio
978-0-470-17474-6

MySpace For Dummies
978-0-470-09529-4

Podcasting For Dummies
978-0-471-74898-4

Search Engine Optimization For Dummies, 2nd Edition
978-0-471-97998-2

Second Life For Dummies
978-0-470-18025-9

Starting an eBay Business For Dummi 3rd Edition†
978-0-470-14924-9

GRAPHICS, DESIGN & WEB DEVELOPMENT

Adobe Creative Suite 3 Design Premium All-in-One Desk Reference For Dummies
978-0-470-11724-8

Adobe Web Suite CS3 All-in-One Desk Reference For Dummies
978-0-470-12099-6

AutoCAD 2008 For Dummies
978-0-470-11650-0

Building a Web Site For Dummies, 3rd Edition
978-0-470-14928-7

Creating Web Pages All-in-One Desk Reference For Dummies, 3rd Edition
978-0-470-09629-1

Creating Web Pages For Dummies, 8th Edition
978-0-470-08030-6

Dreamweaver CS3 For Dummies
978-0-470-11490-2

Flash CS3 For Dummies
978-0-470-12100-9

Google SketchUp For Dummies
978-0-470-13744-4

InDesign CS3 For Dummies
978-0-470-11865-8

Photoshop CS3 All-in-One Desk Reference For Dummies
978-0-470-11195-6

Photoshop CS3 For Dummies
978-0-470-11193-2

Photoshop Elements 5 For Dummie
978-0-470-09810-3

SolidWorks For Dummies
978-0-7645-9555-4

Visio 2007 For Dummies
978-0-470-08983-5

Web Design For Dummies, 2nd Editi
978-0-471-78117-2

Web Sites Do-It-Yourself For Dummi
978-0-470-16903-2

Web Stores Do-It-Yourself For Dummi
978-0-470-17443-2

LANGUAGES, RELIGION & SPIRITUALITY

Arabic For Dummies
978-0-471-77270-5

Chinese For Dummies, Audio Set
978-0-470-12766-7

French For Dummies
978-0-7645-5193-2

German For Dummies
978-0-7645-5195-6

Hebrew For Dummies
978-0-7645-5489-6

Ingles Para Dummies
978-0-7645-5427-8

Italian For Dummies, Audio Set
978-0-470-09586-7

Italian Verbs For Dummies
978-0-471-77389-4

Japanese For Dummies
978-0-7645-5429-2

Latin For Dummies
978-0-7645-5431-5

Portuguese For Dummies
978-0-471-78738-9

Russian For Dummies
978-0-471-78001-4

Spanish Phrases For Dummies
978-0-7645-7204-3

Spanish For Dummies
978-0-7645-5194-9

Spanish For Dummies, Audio Set
978-0-470-09585-0

The Bible For Dummies
978-0-7645-5296-0

Catholicism For Dummies
978-0-7645-5391-2

The Historical Jesus For Dummies
978-0-470-16785-4

Islam For Dummies
978-0-7645-5503-9

Spirituality For Dummies, 2nd Edition
978-0-470-19142-2

NETWORKING AND PROGRAMMING

ASP.NET 3.5 For Dummies
978-0-470-19592-5

C# 2008 For Dummies
978-0-470-19109-5

Hacking For Dummies, 2nd Edition
978-0-470-05235-8

Home Networking For Dummies, 4th Edition
978-0-470-11806-1

Java For Dummies, 4th Edition
978-0-470-08716-9

Microsoft® SQL Server™ 2008 All-in-One Desk Reference For Dummies
978-0-470-17954-3

Networking All-in-One Desk Reference For Dummies, 2nd Edition
978-0-7645-9939-2

Networking For Dummies, 8th Edition
978-0-470-05620-2

SharePoint 2007 For Dummies
978-0-470-09941-4

Wireless Home Networking For Dummies, 2nd Edition
978-0-471-74940-0